P9-DBS-067

SCRAPBOOK STYLES

Ease & Elegance

Two souls
with but
a single
thought

LaBella

Two hearts
that beat
as one

Waterfall

Wishes

SCRAPBOOK STYLES

Ease & Elegance

JILL MILLER

100+ INNOVATIVE IDEAS
FOR
EVERY OCCASION!

WATSON-GUPTILL PUBLICATIONS / NEW YORK

Senior Acquisitions Editor: Joy Aquilino
Edited by Amy Handy
Designed by Georgia Rucker
Graphic production by Hector Campbell
Unless otherwise noted, photographs are by the artist who
created the scrapbook page.

First published in 2004 by Watson-Guptill Publications,
a division of VNU Business Media, Inc.,
770 Broadway, New York, NY 10003
www.watsonguptill.com

Library of Congress Control Number: 2004104991

ISBN 0-8230-1593-9   745.593

Printed in the United States of America

First printing, 2004

1 2 3 4 5 6 7 8 9 / 12 11 10 09 08 07 06 05 04

Ease & Elegance

INTRODUCTION   6

1. **STICKER SURPRISE**   8
Beginner: Small Stickers, Attribute Stickers, Mosaic Sticker Frames
Intermediate: Sticker Scrabble, Distressing Stickers, Faux Metal Frames
Advanced: Lacquered Stickers, Interactive Panels

2. **STENCILING WITH A TWIST**   14
Beginner: Computer Stencils, Decorative Stencils, Lettering as a Design Element
Intermediate: Laser-Cut Title, Stickers as Stencils, Reverse Stencil
Advanced: Sponging, Two-Step Stenciling

3. **DIECUTS AND PUNCH ART**   20
Beginner: Highlighting Diecuts, Layered Punch Art
Intermediate: 3-D Diecuts, Foil Diecuts, Mat Board Diecuts
Advanced: Punched Frames, Dimensional Diecut Frames

4. **SIMPLE AND SOPHISTICATED STAMPING**   26
Beginner: Watermark Stamping, Thermography, Foil Stamping
Intermediate: Bold Watercolor Images, Soft-Shaded Outline, Stamping on Painted Background
Advanced: Stamping Mirror Tiles, Dramatic Ink Stamp

5. **FRAMED AND FANTASTIC**   32
Beginner: Simple Premade Frames, Diecuts as Frames, Customizing Frame Size, Customizing Frames with Color
Intermediate: Heritage-Look Frame, Distressing Embossed Frames, Distressing Cardboard Frames
Advanced: Foil Frames, Sliding Photo Frame

6. **INVITATION-STYLE SCRAPBOOKING**   38
Beginner: Glassine Envelope, Vellum Pockets, Mini Envelopes
Intermediate: Overlapping Windows, Envelope Boxes, Gate Cards
Advanced: Mini Accordion Books, Pillow Pouches

7. **PREPRINTED PAPERS AND COLORBLOCKING**   44
Beginner: Quadrant Layout, Colorblocking, Preprinted Colorwashed Paper
Intermediate: Triangle Pockets, Monochromatic Papers, Paper Weaving
Advanced: Coordinated Sets, Powdered Metallic Colorblocking

8. **HANDMADE AND EMBOSSED PAPERS**   50
Beginner: Window Silhouette, Embossed Motifs, Embossed Leather, Layered Vellum
Intermediate: Brushing Ink on Embossed Paper, Rubbing Ink on Embossed Paper, Painting Embossed Paper
Advanced: Painting with Powders, Painting with Metallic Acrylics

9. **METALLIC TOUCHES**   56
Beginner: Antiquing Cream, Metal Tag Decorations, Paperclip Accents
Intermediate: Metallic Accents, Foil Windows, Creating with Window Screen
Advanced: Mesh with Iridescent Foils, Mesh Collage

10. **GLITTER, GLASS, AND PLASTIC**   62
Beginner: Tumbled Glass, Glitter Snow, Superfine Glitter, Superfine Glitter with Accents
Intermediate: Cracked Faux Glass, Glitter Glue, Pearlized Paint
Advanced: Plastic Wrap Water Effects, Inks on Transparency

11. **PUDDLES AND IMPRESSIONS**   68
Beginner: Hot Glue Stamping, Stamping in Embossing Powder, Wax Seals
Intermediate: Liquid Appliqué, Modeling Paste
Advanced: Faux Weathered Wood, Artist Cement

12. **EXPRESSIONS ART**   74
Beginner: Creative Lettering, Expressions Stickers
Intermediate: Title Borders, Overlapping Text Highlights, Embossing Text
Advanced: Photoshop Effects, More Special Effects

The vast majority of pictures that people scrapbook tend to be formal occasions such as weddings and family portraits, and these photos call for a sense of elegance and sophistication. While these events are important to document, other less formal occasions such as birthdays, back-to-school rituals, and newborn baby celebrations also need to be remembered. Even everyday occurrences like bedtime routines, quirky family traditions, and teenage tantrums are an important part of who we are and what we love, and cannot be left behind in the recollections of our future generations. If our past defines us, we need to honor and embrace it within our scrapbooks. That being said, the task of the family historian may seem too overwhelming to undertake. In *Scrapbook Styles: Ease & Elegance,* I have sought to help lighten the load by providing a multitude of ideas that speak to the busy beginner as well as the seasoned scrapbooker. While I include some traditional approaches to scrapbooking systems, I enjoy tweaking the traditional and sometimes even turning things inside out to create layouts that venture far beyond the typical scrapbook page.

This book is different from other books in the ways it adds clever twists to beginner techniques utilizing basic scrapbooking components such as stickers, stencils, and diecuts. I also developed some unusual approaches to working with frames, envelopes, and all manner of papers. Fresh looks at stamping, antiquing, and metallizing are also found within these pages. And finally, to throw a curve in your creativity, I've included some out-of-the-ordinary embellishments such as glass, plastic, and iridescent glitter, paints, and foils.

Because I wanted to cram these pages full of new ideas, I give little attention to the rudimentary basics such as cropping and affixing photos to the page. A great many books are available to learn about scrapbooking fundamentals. This book focuses instead on expanding your creative spirit while it acknowledges that many of us are consumed by other demands and have little time for complicated instructions. Each chapter offers projects in three categories: Beginner, for new scrapbookers or those seeking quick-to-assemble projects; Intermediate, for those with a bit more time and/or experience; and Advanced, for cutting-edge souls who like a gentle challenge. Thus, whatever your skill level, you can jump right in and try out a vast array of interesting techniques. Another feature scattered throughout these pages are small sidebars offering hints at alternative approaches. "Subject Switch" suggests other themes that could work with the title in question, and "Title Twist" lists other titles that might complement the theme under discussion.

While we love the look of sepiatones and black-and-whites, most of us tend to embrace color wholeheartedly. The projects in this book are absolutely filled with color. With that in mind, a quick conversation about choosing colors for your pictures is necessary. In almost all cases, try to draw from the colors within your photographs. If you find that the photos have loud hues that you do not care for, convert those photos to black-and-whites or sepiatones to quiet the colors into a monochromatic palette. The same can also be done with photos that have distracting backgrounds. Recognize that the colors of your world are a part of your life's experiences and need to be passed on along with your thoughts and artistic expressions to your children's children.

I am thrilled to bring you *Scrapbook Styles: Ease & Elegance*. I enjoyed creating the art within it and hope you enjoy creating your own art from it.

CHAPTER 1

Sticker Surprise

Ever wonder how to jazz up stickers so they don't "float" off their pages or simply get lost in the crowd of components? In this chapter we will examine some basic as well as advanced techniques to add impact and elegance to a wide variety of stickers. Whether simple or sophisticated, large or small, I'm going to show you how to dress things up, cut things up, and mix things up! Get set to see these supply list basics in a whole new light.

Small Stickers

"I See Red" shows how grouping small stickers together into shapes and titles will give visual weight to an otherwise insignificant embellishment.

I See Red
Artist: Jill Miller
Photographer: David Thornell
All vellum stickers, stamps, papers: Printworks

SUBJECT SWITCH
- Blushing Brides
- Boo-Boo Pages
- Christmas Themes
- Red-Headed Beauties
- Valentine's Day

Attribute Stickers

"U.S.A. Play" makes use of attribute stickers—sensitive, creative, smart, and so on—along with some clever wordplay with the title, for a fast and easy tribute to my youngest son.

U.S.A. Play
Artist: Jill Miller
All stickers and panorama photos:
Creative Imaginations
Circle tags: Making Memories
Fabric stars: Jewelcraft

Mosaic Sticker Frames

Place stickers on grid paper and then cut them into tiles to create decorative and elegant photo or journaling frames.

❀ Adhere a sticker frame centered on a 3 x 8-inch panel of mosaic grid paper.

❀ Cut sticker-frame squares from grid, removing excess white along top and bottom of frame.

❀ Spread sticker-frame squares evenly apart, following photo size as shown. Center photograph in frame.

❀ Repeat steps to make larger frame using border stickers. Overlap border stickers at frame corners. Miter-cut corners and remove excess sticker.

TITLE TWIST
- Along the Road Less Traveled
- The Journey of 1,000 Miles
- My Big Backyard
- Scouting with the Scouts
- A Walk in the Woods

Spring
Artist: Jill Miller
Daisy Vines embossed papers, vellums, stickers: K and Company
White mosaic grid paper: Diecuts with a View

Sticker Scrabble

"Christmas Scrabble" plays off the ever-popular board game, and almost any theme or occasion can be handled the same way. Easily recognizable words like "Happy Birthday" or "Valentine's Day" fit this layout particularly well. To create your own word scrabble, trim your photo(s) to fit within a sticker unit, or close enough to compensate for the spacing with the photo mat. If you need ideas for a variety of layouts, try using a computer Scrabble game, or even rearranging real Scrabble tiles.

Christmas Scrabble
Jill Miller
All stickers: K and Company
Specialty paper: Creative Imaginations

Distressing Stickers

Believe it or not, sandpaper and stickers do mix, as you can see in Cary Oliver's "Freedom For All." and that's not all we distress. Look closely and you'll see that as well as the stickers, the edges of the photos have also been swiped with sandpaper, adding to the overall vintage-chic appeal of the collage.

Freedom for All
Artist: Cary Oliver
Specialty paper and stickers: Provo Craft
Other: Fine sandpaper (for photo edges and sticker), embroidery floss

Faux Metal Frames

For my grandfather's gang of WWII engineers, I used metallic rub-ons to conjure up a faux metal frame placed against a map background.

- The sticker frame panel comes with two decorative frames and one plain one. Remove the two decorative frames from the backing and mount on the photos. Lightly crinkle plain frame and apply metallic rub-ons before separating it from backing.

- Repeat crinkle-and-rub technique on tags and wall map, then tear tags and use the punch to create tag window.

LaBella Engineer
Artist: Jill Miller
Frame stickers: Mrs. Grossman
Metallic rub-ons: Craf-T Products
Wall map: Staples
Specialty paper: Carolee's Creations
Tags: Avery
1½-inch square punch: Marvy

Beauties From the Past

I had these pictures taken of Morgan and Piper for a Father's Day gift to their Daddy. They had such a good time getting dressed up and posing so perfectly for their Daddy. They came out so beautiful that you would believe that they actually are living in this old fashioned time and not in the new millennium, 2000.

Lacquered Stickers

Crystal Lacquer adds a bit of clear finish to any sticker in much the same way as clear nail polish adds highlights to our hands. In "Beauties from the Past" this glasslike effect both enhances the vellum and lends sparkling highlights to the stickers.

- Use Crystal Lacquer to highlight the roses and leaves on the diecuts. Allow a minimum of 30 minutes to dry.

- With decorative scissors, trim inside of oval vellum photo mat and outside edge of coordinating vellum. Adhere with foam tape.

Beauties from the Past
Artist: Shawne Osterman
Paper, stickers, diecuts, vellum: K and Company
Crystal lacquer: Sakura Industries
Victorian decorative scissors: Fiskars
Font: Lettering Delights Girly Curls
Other: Foam tape, sheer ribbon

Twins with Roses

Artist: Jill Miller

Photographer: David Thornell

Green and pink vellums: Autumn leaves

Specialty paper, embossed stickers, letters: K and Company

Birch leaf punch: Marvy Uchida

Other: Photo-safe tape, pink cardstock

Interactive Panels

In "Twins with Roses," interactive border sticker panels open to reveal many cherished childhood memories of me with my twin sister Stacey.

♡ Seam together two sheets of specialty paper with tape on back side of paper and trim off 1 inch. Fold in each side at 7 inches from outer edge, back over again at 3 inches, leaving 4-inch panel on each side. If desired, fasten inside surfaces of these panels together so that there is just a single flap to open on each side. Center on pink cardstock.

♡ Enlarge and print photo in black and white onto green vellum for photo mat.

♡ Punch out leaves from green vellum and crunch them to add dimension. Adhere all elements as shown.

TITLE TWIST

- Best Buds (floral pages)
- Hand in Hand
- My Buddy, My Brother
- My Sweet Sister
- Together Forever

Time to dust off your stencils! Stencils are one of the most underappreciated design tools, despite the fact that they are sold everywhere and are easy to master. In this chapter we will explore techniques that use stencils in unique applications, starting with premade stencil and easy-to-make computer-lettering stencils, as well as faux stencil looks with vinyl stickers, reverse stenciling with wet transfer and masking stickers, and two-step stenciling processes.

Computer Stencils

Custom stencils from your computer are surprisingly easy. Simply print your text on cardstock and cut it out with a craft knife to create a stencil with which to use ink, paint, or colored pencil to decorate your pages. In "I Love You," Sheila Doherty printed the word "love" on cardstock in reverse, cut out the letters, turned them over, and applied them directly to the page, thereby eliminating the need for coloring tools and extra steps.

SUBJECT SWITCH

· Consider adapting this to a humorous application instead of a serious expression of sentiment.

I Love You
Artist: Sheila Doherty
Specialty paper: Paper Adventures
Chunky glitter: Soft Flex Company
Crystal sticker: Mark Richards Enterprises
Font: Scriptina, 2 Peas Gingersnap
Other: Cardstock, craft knife

Stenciling with a Twist

Decorative Stencils

Applying paint through a stencil is true traditional stenciling, although the use of paint pens adds a little twist. This look is especially beautiful in metallics, as can be seen in "Vienna." The abstract architectural quality of the large photo makes a striking backdrop to the smaller scene, and the coins, stamps, and map are wonderful mementos of Cary's Austrian travels.

Vienna
Artists: Cary Oliver, Jill Miller
Specialty paper: Far and Away
Shadowbox frame: Creative
Imaginations
Decorative stencil: Delta
Gold and copper metallic paint
pens: Marvy Uchida
Other: Brass hinge, mini flip-style
photo album

Storm Soccer
Artist: Jill Miller
Photography: Shooting Stars Photography
Clear transparency: Avery
Lettering stencil, specialty paper: Wordsworth
Yellow vellum: NRN Designs
Other: Black cardstock

Lettering as a Design Element

"Storm Soccer" cuts away letters from transparencies and vellum using a stylized alphabet stencil. The bold, graphic look is very striking, yet the actual technique is quite simple.

- Print your photos on clear transparency sheets and rip away edges of paper backing.

- Trace letters from stencil in reverse on black cardstock and cut out. Adhere some letters as shown along with center photo onto yellow vellum. With same stencil, cut out relevant accent words from photo and vellum, allowing background paper to show through.

- Adhere remaining photos and letters as shown.

Laser-Cut Title

A laser-cut stencil was used to create the title lettering seen here. The vibrant green of the grass in the photo, echoed in the lettering and in the interior spaces of the vinyl sticker, helps to create a lively summer page. The overlaid clear vellum mutes the plaid and makes the photo pop even more. At first glance the butterflies appeared to be made with a traditional stencil technique and then outlined in silver (as has been done with the title), but the silver outline is actually a vinyl sticker whose interiors have simply been filled in.

Ben's Summer
Artist: Jill Miller
Photographer: Robyn Thornell
Summer plaid vellum and clear vellum:
Autumn Leaves
Dragonfly Class A Peals: Stampendous
Summer title block: Deluxe Cuts
Yellow, spring green, emerald green, orange,
silver, and blue Twinklette markers: Marvy
Metal tags: Avery

Stickers as Stencils

Cool-hued metallic paints and silver vinyl stickers are featured in "Warm Winter Wishes." Sponging over and around removable stickers is a fast way to add fantastic shimmer and shine to this clean, classic layout.

- Fold and mask one-third of cardstock along left edge and arrange two-thirds of snowflake stickers randomly on the page.
- Pump metallic paint from pens into each sponge and sponge left side panel with both colors. Gently remove painted snowflakes.
- Sponge silver paint on scrap white cardstock for larger photo mat and mount as shown. Reposition painted snowflakes around white side of page and affix unpainted snowflakes on left side panel as shown. Arrange lettering stickers on scrap white cardstock strip and adhere to page with mini brads.

Warm Winter Wishes
Artist: Jill Miller
Photographer: David Thornell
Metallic stickers: Stampendous
Blue and silver metallic paint pens: Marvy Uchida
Metal circle tag: Avery
Other: white cardstock, 2 kitchen sponges, silver mini brads

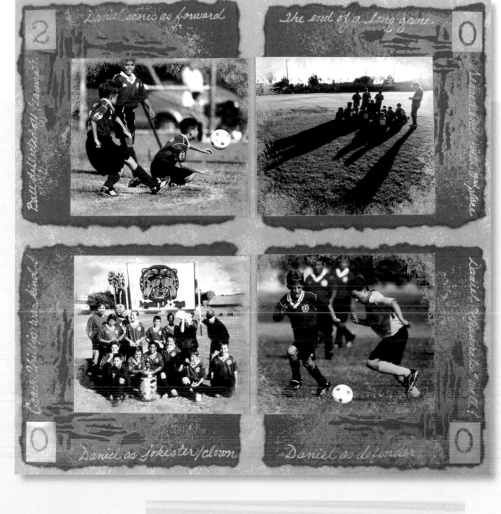

Reverse Stencil

Reverse stenciling is certainly a twist on tradition, as is evident in "Maddog Soccer." Close examination reveals a reverse stencil technique that must be seen, and executed, to be believed.

☆ Tear blue cardstock into four 5½-inch squares. Sponge gold ink over stencil onto another sheet of cardstock (save this for a future layout), then mist stencil with water. Lay one blue square over wet stencil and firmly rub wet stencil to transfer ink to corner of square. Repeat with remaining three squares.

☆ After blue squares, photographs, and number stickers are affixed to page, sponge gold ink on edges of photos, numbers, and cardstock as shown.

Maddog Soccer
Artist: Jill Miller
Photographer: Shooting Stars Photography
Moss green and indigo blue cardstock: Club Scrap
Gold Brilliance ink pad: Tsukineko
Moody Blues stencil, number stickers: Club Scrap
Other: Kitchen sponge, spray bottle

Sponging

People are naturally curious, so interactive pages that let us peek behind or lift the flaps have strong appeal. Both this project and the next feature similar construction and sponge painting techniques for very different looks. Refer to page 13 for specifics on creating an interactive page.

☾ Seam together two pieces of 12 x 12-inch paper. Fold each side into middle, then fold back each side in half again, following directions on page 13.

☾ Affix a wave border sticker on right front panel. Sponge all three colors of Lumiere paints over entire panel, including sticker. (Open panels and lay page face down to avoid painting inside center section.) This reverse stencil technique uses the sticker as a mask to keep background paper free from paint and thus creates dramatic contrasted images against the painted surfaces.

☾ Lift off sticker and place it on left front panel. Repeat sponging and sticker lift-off process. Set sticker aside.

☾ Place sticker greetings in the four corners of 5½ x 8½-inch white cardstock rectangle and lightly sponge with paint. Adhere photo on green cardstock and painted cardstock as shown. Carefully remove stickers with tweezers and place on edges of purple cardstock as shown.

☾ Cut wave border sticker into sections and place between photos as shown. Sponge a second wave border sticker if necessary to span gaps.

Christmas Tree Hunt
Artist: Jill Miller
Halo Violet Gold, Bright Gold, and Metallic Olive Green Lumiere acrylic paints: Jacquard Products
Class A Peels holiday greetings, wave border stickers: Stampendous
Other: Specialty paper, white cardstock, purple cardstock, 3 kitchen sponges, tweezers, photo mat

Two-Step Stenciling

"Kevin" uses two-step stenciling with metallic paint pens to create another appealing open-and-shut page. Please refer to directions on page 13 for specifics on making interactive elements.

- Pump green metallic paint into a kitchen sponge and lightly sponge through stencil randomly on vellum. Repeat with blue on second section of stencil, overlapping green images.

- Repeat the process to make two butterflies on scrap white cardstock, let dry for a minute, and cut out. Cover each butterfly with glue stick and lay folded vellum expression cutout on top of each butterfly cutout as shown, making sure vellum fold is just inside fold of each cardstock panel.

- Silhouette-cut corner butterflies on vellum to form photo corners.

- Punch tags with dragonfly motif, thread silver cording through tags, and wrap cording around each panel, tucking vellum expression under each side as shown. Mount remaining elements with glue stick or metal clips as shown.

Kevin

Artist: Jill Miller
Photographer: Anita Shell Photography
Specialty paper, butterfly stencil, lettering stickers: Club Scrap
Green and blue metallic paint pens, dragonfly punch: Marvy
Tags, metal clips: Avery
Clear vellum, vellum expressions: Memories Complete
Other: White cardstock, 2 kitchen sponges, glue stick, silver elastic cording

CHAPTER 3

Diecuts and Punch Art

Diecuts seem to have been around forever. Long ago, scrapbookers were limited to stealing time in school supply closets to cut a few diecuts for their personal use along with those they cut for their children's classes. Over the years many, many techniques have been developed for these products, and as they have evolved so must our thinking about the possible uses for these scrapbooking staples. Along with the introduction of some tried-and-true applications of diecuts and punches, we will also explore ways to distress, collage, interlock, and dimensionalize, and to add movement, metallic highlights, and soft watercolor edges to all sizes and shapes of these wonderful accents.

Highlighting Diecuts

Simple diecuts dressed up with glitter glues and crystal lacquer add a touch of class to this celebration spread.

☆ Pierce end of Crystal Lacquer and carefully pour small lines of lacquer along highlights of each sticker. Repeat process with glitter glues. Depending on thickness of applications, allow 30 minutes or more for lacquer and glues to dry.

☆ Thread a small piece of ribbon through a picture hanger to give the illusion that photo is hanging on the page.

Christmas Memories
Artists: Shawne Osterman, Jill Miller
Paper, stickers, frames, border diecuts: K and Company
Crystal Lacquer: Sakura
Other: Ribbon, glitter glues, brads, picture hanger

Layered Punch Art

With the invention of punches, scrapbookers could begin to experiment with repeated designs or distressing techniques without incurring significant costs. Cary Oliver has done just that with "Autumn," supplementing the title with added color, piling on the crumpled leaves, and slightly distressing the edges of the photos.

🍂 Punch out desired letters. To give them color, affix letters to cardstock with repositionable tape. Holding three brush markers tightly together, run the points across letters. Repeat with another three colors on remaining portions of letters. Mount letters on strip of ecru vellum.

🍂 Before arranging photos, sand edges to add interest.

🍂 Mount leather straps to the page with brads.

🍂 Punch out cardstock leaves in several colors. To increase the rustic appeal, crumple leaves and scatter around page and over photos. Place large grouping of leaves on top of straps on left side and adhere title on top.

Autumn
Artist: Cary Oliver
Letter punches: eA-Zy Punch System, Scrapsakes
Leaf punch, brush markers: Marvy
Ecru vellum: Printworks
Other: Brown, rust, red, green, and yellow cardstock; mini brads, leather straps, sandpaper

3-D Diecuts

A few years ago, three-dimensional stickers hit the market. Within a year, 3D stickers began featuring all sorts of accents, including wires, buttons, and fabric. Coordinating sets, as seen in Cary Oliver's "Graduation," are just the tip of the iceberg. Dimension and interest can also be added with foam diecuts and mat board.

☆ Add smoky gray chalk accents around edges of all tags and journal.

☆ Align top and bottom border diecuts and thread title plate, matted photos, and sliding tags across page with thin silver cording as shown. Secure ends of cording on back of page.

Graduation
Artist: Cary Oliver
Photographer: Shaun Austin Photography
Stitched paper, 3D diecuts, tags, borders: Westrim
Other: Gray chalk, silver cording, silver eyelets

Ian Growing Up
Artist: Jill Miller
Red and gold foils: Amaco
Heart diecut: Sizzix Ellison
Specialty paper: Autumn Leaves
Gold mesh: Magic Scraps

Foil Diecuts

As "Ian Growing Up" demonstrates, diecut systems allow scrapbookers to cut shapes easily from foil, as well as from burlap, leather, and other unusual materials. Since the metal frame of a diecut plate is ⅛ inch thick and is compressed with heavy pressure by virtue of a pull-down arm, a wide variety of thick or very thin and flexible material can be cut with a diecut machine.

♡ Diecut hearts from foils and remove centers. Lay out hearts on paper and weave strip of mesh through centers. Cut letters for title from red foil.

♡ Mount scraps of gold foil and mesh behind photos.

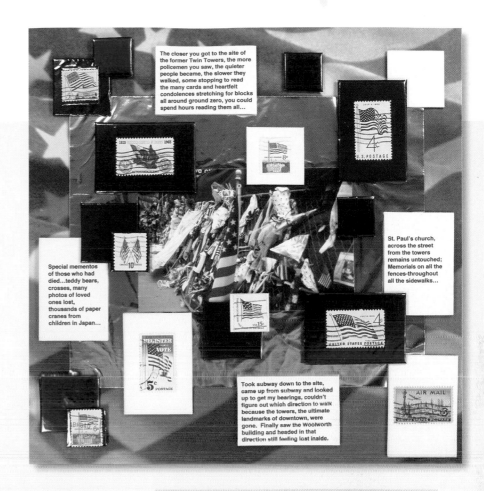

Mat Board Diecuts

For an effective multilayered quilt-style page, "Twin Towers" utilizes mat board diecuts wrapped with red, silver, and blue foils. Silhouetted against the foils, canceled postage stamps featuring United States flags echo the flags in the photo and combine with moving commentaries to create a very memorable image.

∅ Cut foils slightly larger than mat board diecuts and adhere to diecut fronts. Trim foil corners at a 45-degree angle and wrap foil around diecut edges; secure on back.

∅ Affix postage stamps to some of the foil-wrapped diecuts.

∅ Arrange elements on page and use foam tape to create different levels, overlapping edges as shown.

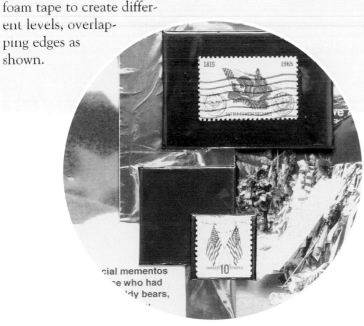

Twin Towers

Artist: Jill Miller

Photographer: Robyn Dellamura

Red, silver, and blue foil: Amaco

Mat board diecuts: www.thecardladies.com

Specialty paper: Wubie Prints

Other: canceled postage stamps, foam tape

SUBJECT SWITCH

This layout with the journaled squares lends itself to various themes:

- Family tree
- Important dates of the year
- List of birthday or holiday presents
- Travelogues

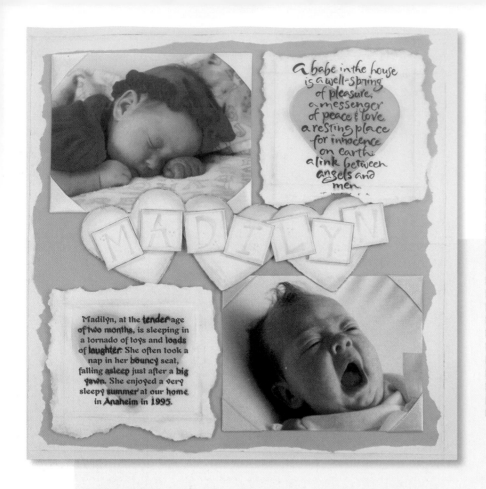

A babe in the house
is a well-spring
of pleasure,
a messenger
of peace & love,
a resting place
for innocence
on earth;
a link between
angels and
men.

Madilyn, at the tender age
of two months, is sleeping in
a tornado of toys and loads
of laughter. She often took a
nap in her bouncy seat,
falling asleep just after a big
yawn. She enjoyed a very
sleepy summer at our home
in Anaheim in 1995.

Madilyn
Artist: Jill Miller
Photographer: Anita
Shell Photography
Pink Twinklette marker, color-
less blender pen, Giga heart
punch: Marvy Uchida
Embossed lettering squares:
What's New, Ltd.
Printable clear vellum (greet-
ing card pack): Avery
Expression sticker:
Wordsworth Stamps
Other: Cardstock, plastic
plate, foam tape, craft knife,
wet wipes (optional), white
and pink satin ribbons

Punched Frames

A few basic shaped punches and an assortment of diecut frames are absolutely essential to any scrapbooker's stash. A simple heart punch lends itself to almost any theme. If the punch is large enough you can use both the heart and the interior punched hole to create a heart-shaped frame, as seen in "Madilyn."

⑥ Cut a piece of 8½ x 11-inch white cardstock in half, for two 5½ x 8½-inch rectangles. Fold each rectangle in half again so finished size measures 5½ x 4¼ inches.

⑥ Punch a heart in center of each rectangle, with bottom of heart just above fold. Open fold and tear along cardstock *below* fold. Crease remaining three sides of rectangle and tear edges.

⑥ Scribble pink Twinklette marker on a plastic plate and pick up color with blender pen. Watercolor with blender pen around each heart-shaped hole, around creases, and around three of the heart punch-outs, refreshing plastic plate and blender pen with color as needed. Repeat watercolor effects on letters and letter squares. If you cannot find a blender pen, use a wet wipe (although colors will be less vibrant).

⑥ Print journaling and accent words with pink marker on back of printed vellum. Affix journaling and sticker to punched white cardstock squares. Add vellum to back of expression sticker and mount frames with foam tape as shown. Wrap small pieces of ribbon around photo corners and secure to back of photo.

TITLE TWIST
• Angel
• Perfect
• Precious
• Princess/Prince

Dimensional Diecut Frames

The rectangular frames in "Sand, Swim, and Sun" are diecut from wavy corrugated paper and highlighted with metallic rub-ons. Once again both the frame and the center section are used in this "swing-out style" scrapbook page.

⚓ Diecut five wavy blue and five wavy white rectangle frames. Add sapphire blue and silver metallic rub-ons to blue frames. Spray with fixative.

⚓ Punch holes in one pair of opposite corners in each frame and set eyelets in holes. Punch holes for silver brads in a third corner of each frame. Align white frames with blue frames and punch brad hole into white frames.

⚓ Mount background wave photo print paper on teal cardstock. Lay frames on mounted papers and punch brad hole through background papers; secure frames to page with star brads. Adhere blue frames to background paper under opposite corners with foam tape.

⚓ Mount photos on back of white rectangles that were punched out of frames in first step. Insert mounted photos into blue corrugated frames. Insert blue rectangles into center of white frames and add journaling. Add seashells to lower corners of each white frame. Do not fully secure the offset white frames; this allows them to pivot open to expose journaling.

Sand, Swim, and Sun
Artist: Jill Miller
Rectangular frame Sizzix diecut: Ellison
White and blue wavy corrugated paper: Paper Reflections
Sapphire blue and silver metallic rub-ons: Craf-T Products
4 star brads, 16 silver eyelets, hole punch, eyelet setter: Stamp Studio
12 x 12-inch photo print paper in wave design: Wubie paper
Blue Twinklettes glitter pen: Marvy Uchida
Blue threads, tiny seashells: Magic Scraps
Other: Spray fixative, teal cardstock

SUBJECT SWITCH

Try seasonal subjects with this technique:

- Summer: Hot, Long, Lazy
- Fall: Crisp, Chilly, Bright
- Winter: Frozen, White, Still
- Spring: New, Fresh, Green

advanced

Stamping is a craft that has been practiced for ages, even longer than scrapbooking has, so a marriage between these two crafts can produce classic pieces of art. Simple stamping incorporates tone-on-tone effects and black outline images, while sophisticated stamping involves the use of solvent-based inks on mirror tiles and iron transfers that "crush" images into velveteen. To learn these techniques, as well as many in between these extremes, follow the advice on these pages and open your mind to the wonderful possibilities of stamping for your scrapbook pages.

Watermark Stamping

Employing handmade paper that has been stamped with watermark ink and embossed with clear powder, "Fishing Dreams" features the subtle suggestion of stylized leaves on the paper. Watermark ink is a clear ink that darkens the paper color, producing a tone-on-tone image.

- Ink, stamp, and emboss bold birch leaf with watermark ink and clear embossing powder on handmade papers, definition journaling block, and beige cardstock.
- Adhere vellum journaling over leaf image with glue stick and add photos, metal frames, and paper strips as shown.

Fishing Dreams
Artist: Jill Miller
Leaf stamp, embossing powder: Stampendous
Watermark ink: VersaMark Tsukineko
Handmade paper: Creative Imaginations
Metal frames, photo corners, word definitions: Making Memories

Thermography

"A Home of Our Own" is easy to create because I "cheated" with the use of thermography paper, a paper that has been stamped and embossed during its manufacture. As such it is "good to go" straight from the store. Scrapbookers rejoice!

❧ Rub sapphire blue and copper metallic rub-ons randomly into thermography paper as shown. Remove excess color from embossed designs with dry tissue. Repeat with four diecut frames as shown.

❧ Fold one frame in half each way, reducing size to 4 x 4-inch square. Add copper brads at each fold and turn on point. Silhouette-cut designs as shown and adhere all frames, adding foam tape under middle frame. Cut apart expression sticker and add to frames.

❧ Diecut tags, affix stickers, and trim off excess. Add all copper brads. Secure tags with foam tape. String threads on page as shown.

A Home of Our Own
Artist: Jill Miller
Photographer: Brett South
Architecture thermography paper, tag stickers: Club Scrap
Sapphire blue and copper metallic rub-ons: Craf-T Products
Rectangle frame diecut: Sizzix Ellison
Expressions sticker: Wordsworth
Other: Tissue, mini copper brads, embroidery floss

Foil Stamping

"Susan and Jeffery" uses foil that has been stamped with solvent inks and cut into heart shapes. The inks are permanent and allow the image to be cut from the foil without smearing any lines.

❀ Ink heart stamp with any color permanent ink and stamp on silver foil. Cut out, turn over, and interlace foil hearts as shown. Affix expression sticker to clear vellum and trim off excess.

❀ Adhere expression to landscape portion of photo with double-stick tape. The vellum under the sticker will mute the underlying photo, allowing text of expression to read through images. Adhere remaining elements as desired.

Susan and Jeffery
Artist: Jill Miller
Photographer: Robert Wagner
Curly heart stamp: Printworks
Silver foil: Amaco
Specialty paper: Faux Memories
Silver printed vellum: Colorbok
Expression sticker: Wordsworth
Other: Ink (any color), double-stick tape, scrap cardstock

Irish Blessing
Artist: Jill Miller
Photographer: Anita
Shell Photography
*Pink, purple, emerald
green, orange, and yellow
Twinklette markers: Marvy
Uchida
Large foam rubber leaf
stamp: Rubber Stampede
Expression sticker:
Wordsworth Stamps
Other: Fine-mist spray bot-
tle, oatmeal cardstock,
ivory cardstock, scissors,
plum organza ribbon, pur-
ple and green papers, gold
gel pen*

Bold Watercolor Images

Strongly hued to softly shaded autumn leaves fall beautifully all over "Irish Blessing." Surprisingly, misting with water is an integral part of creating this composition.

- For background paper, color leaf stamp completely with random scribbles of each marker, working from darker colors out to yellow on tips of leaf (color will be very light on stamp).

- *Lightly* mist stamp with water and stamp it on oatmeal cardstock. Mist leaf again and stamp again. Continue misting and stamping until leaf image is very light on cardstock. Refresh stamp with markers, mist and stamp again, repeating until paper is covered with leaves. Color, mist, and stamp journaling block as shown, working from center image out. Place expression sticker over leaf-stamped rectangle.

- Accordion-fold a 9¾ x 4½-inch rectangle of ivory cardstock into thirds (finished size should be 3¼ inches long by 4½ inches high). Color, mist, and stamp leaf in center of front panel of accordion book, making sure to keep one edge of stamp along fold. (You will be cutting out around leaf shape and you'll want the three leaves to stay attached, like paper dolls.) Mist and stamp second panel and repeat with last panel. Fold book closed and trim around leaf image with very sharp scissors, making sure to keep portions of each fold intact so stamped leaves don't separate from each other.

- Mount organza ribbon to page and attach bottom of leaf booklet over ribbon. Tie book closed with ribbon. Mount photo on wavy-cut purple and green papers, edge with gold gel pen, and adhere remaining elements to page.

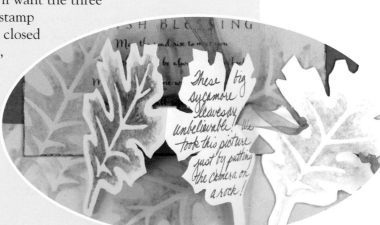

Soft-Shaded Outline

The age-old but sometimes tricky art of watercolor painting is made more approachable with the use of brush art markers and a wet cotton swab. This technique is especially effective with embossed images, because the raised embossing keeps the separate marker colors from blurring together while maintaining a strong, clean outline.

☾ Stamp image on cardstock and title on envelope, and emboss. For soft watercolor effects, draw with art markers only around outline of images and title and blend color into center with wet cotton swab.

☾ For larger swatch of faded color, as on photo panels, apply marker to baby wipe and gently swipe wipe over desired sections. To highlight other elements, brush markers along edges of panels and heart diecuts. Attach bear and balloons with foam tape as shown.

☾ Adhere heart-shaped photos on heart diecuts and journal on reverse of diecut. Insert hearts into glassine envelopes and secure to page.

Somebear New
Artist: Jill Miller
All stamps, glassine envelopes: Stampington & Company
Black ink, embossing powder: Colorbox
Violet, yellow, and teal Brush Art markers: Marvy
Specialty paper: Provo Craft
Other: Cardstock, cotton swabs, baby wipes

Emily's Sour Face
Artist: Jill Miller
Metallic russet and halo blue gold Lumiere paints: Jacquard Products
Lace background stamp: Stampin' Up!
White Brilliance ink: Tsukineko
Expression sticker: Serendipity
Other: White cardstock, 2-inch wide foam brush, lace ribbon (two 13-inch pieces)

Stamping on Painted Background

When white cardstock is painted with bold blocks of color and then a white background pattern is stamped over the dried paint, the white stamped image appears clearly only on the areas of color. Thus the effect is one of bold color broken by random patterns, lending drama to the composition.

♡ With foam brush, swipe paints onto areas of white cardstock. Let dry, then stamp lace background image.

♡ From cardstock, cut rectangle slightly larger than expression sticker and mount sticker in opening as shown. Mount photo on white cardstock and adhere to page.

♡ Position ribbon on page as shown and secure ends on back of page. Journal on thin strip of white cardstock and adhere between ribbons.

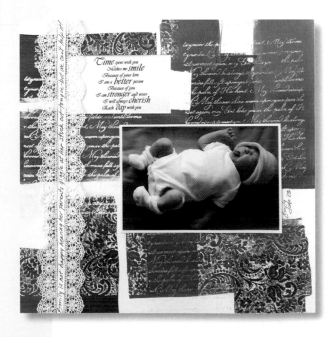

Fishwish
Artist: Jill Miller
*Bag of 1/2-inch mirror tiles
(32 total), fish stamp: Plaid
Ultramarine, forest green, and
azure StaZon inks: Tsukineko
Fantastix (3), sponge daubers
(3): Tsukineko
Grid overlay: DieCuts with a View
Artextures preprinted paper,
silver paper: Paper Adventures
Lettering stickers: Chyops
Other: Masking tape, 3 kitchen
sponges, double-stick tape,
foam tape*

Stamping Mirror Tiles

Traditionally, nonporous surfaces such as mirrors were taboo when it came to stamping because they would repel the color, but solvent inks make it possible to adorn these kinds of surfaces. In "Fishwish," tiny mirror tiles stamped with fish complement the reflective surface of the water and my own little fish, who goes by the name of Ian.

- Arrange 32 mirror tiles into two squares of 16 tiles each. Tape tiles together on back with masking tape. Ink each area of fish stamp with chosen color, transferring ink from pad to stamp with Fantastix stubs (a type of foam blending stub). Stamp multicolored fish on tile fronts as shown. Fill in voids with additional ink as desired, using stubs directly on mirror tiles.

- Sponge grid overlay randomly with inks and remove prepunched squares. Affix photos to background paper and position grid over them. Secure grid border with double-stick tape.

- Remove masking tape from mirror tiles, space tiles slightly apart in groups of four on silver paper as shown, and adhere tiles to silver paper. Mount silver paper/mirror tile assembly on background paper and grid as shown.

- Trim 1-inch squares removed from grid overlay to frame tile mosaic and secure to background paper with foam tape as shown.

advanced

Dramatic Ink Stamp

Ink plays a major role in the Asian-inspired stamped scrapbook page "Looking Ahead." The high-contrast combination of vibrant blue and stark black makes for a striking image. The classic center-stage window has four flaps that have been folded back and rubbed with vibrant blue ink, producing a faux-suede finish.

∅ To make center window, fold specialty paper diagonally in both directions. Open paper and lay flat. With craft knife and straight edge, cut 8-inch slits on folds, 4 inches each way from center cross hairs, to form an X in page center.

∅ Fold back flaps formed by these cuts and apply blue ink with sponge dauber. Repeat with white scroll border. Stamp Asian sayings in black on each flap.

∅ Cut 5½-inch square out of center of 8½-inch square of black cardstock, and trim off corners with decorative scissors. Slip over window flaps formed in first step, secure with tape, and fold flaps back down over black cardstock. String silver cording around corners on black cardstock as shown.

∅ Cut center grill from black grid paper and mount into window over photo. Stamp small silver squares with Asian symbols and mount on page with foam tape as shown.

Looking Ahead
Artist: Jill Miller
Photographer: Stacey Thornell
Specialty paper with preprinted border: What's New, Ltd.
Black and blue VersaFine inks, sponge daubers: Tsukineko
Asian stamp sets: Stampendous
Victorian decorative corner scissors: Fiskars
Black grid photo frame: Diecuts with a View
Other: Craft knife, straight edge, black cardstock, shiny silver squares, silver cording, foam tape

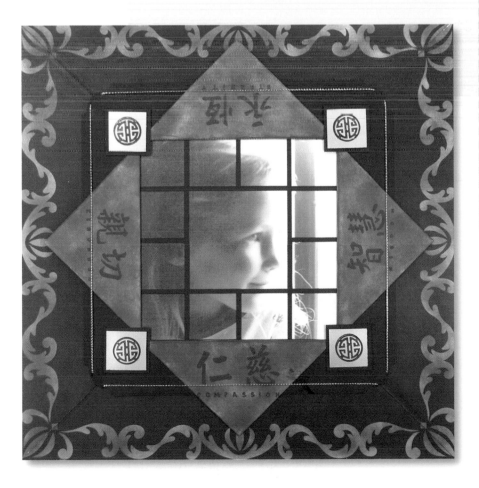

TITLE TWIST
Although this page has no title, try these:
• Dream/Believe
• Possibilities
• Reflections
• Serenity

Once, only prom pictures were packaged with paper premade frames. Luckily, many manufacturers have designed a wide variety of premade frames that provide quick and easy accents, since formal photos are not the only ones deserving of frames. If fun and frolic fill your daily life, celebrate your good fortune by framing those memories on your scrapbook pages. Only one formal portrait is featured in this chapter; all the rest "frame" the familiar day-to-day delights of life with loved ones, encouraging us to focus on the simple joys of family.

Morgan and Aunt Jennifer
Artists: Shawne Osterman,
Jill Miller
All papers, frames, stickers:
Printworks
Brads: American Tag Company
Other: Fabric bag, ribbon

Simple Premade Frames

Both "Morgan and Aunt Jennifer" and "Pretty in Pink" are straightforward examples of two very different kinds of premade frames. The whimsical frames used here offer a lovely complement to the colors and poses in the photos.

Diecuts as Frames

♡ Secure mini photos in windows of three diecut tags. Bond and seal dried flowers to tags with crystal lacquer. Adhere all tags with petals as shown.

♡ Add tile stickers and top with lettering stickers as shown. Journal in window spaces of right-side tags. Adhere main photo.

Pretty in Pink
Artist: Jill Miller
Photographer: Kim Meyer
Specialty papers and lettering stickers: SEI
Diecut tags: DMD Industries
Tile stickers: Sticko/EK Success
Other: Pressed flowers

Customizing Frame Size

Customizing premade frames might seem a bit tricky, but "Daniel 2002" and "Christmas '63" show a couple of approachable ways to do this.

- To reduce size of premade frame, cut across midsection and overlap edges. Hide overlaps with cross bands of paper and ribbon as shown, or with other decorative accents.

- To enlarge premade frame, cut across midsection and spread the two sections apart. Hide gap with strips of paper, bands of ribbon, stickers, diecuts, or other decorative accents.

- Offset middle photo on upper band of page and tuck right and left photos under upper ribbon band and over lower ribbon band as shown. Add title to oval bookplate with gold pen and adhere with foam tape.

Daniel 2002
Artist: Jill Miller
All papers, frame: Anna Griffin
Metallic bookplate frame sticker: Stampendous
Other: Ribbon, gold gel pen

Christmas '63
Artist: Jill Miller
Photographer: David Thornell
Corrugated frame: DMD Industries
Gamma green Brilliance ink pad: Tsukineko
Specialty paper, vellum: Autumn Leaves
Mulberry paper: Carolee's Creations
Banner stencil: C-Thru Ruler
Other: Mini brads, gold pen, postage stamps, foam tape, gold thread

Customizing Frames with Color

To color ridges of corrugated paper, brush frame lightly with ink pad in vertical strokes. For a variation on this technique, try brushing two or three colors on frame.

- Brush gamma green Brilliance ink across surface of precut corrugated window frame, highlighting all ridges. Secure photo to frame back. Add mini brads and small torn squares of tan paper as shown.

- Trim vellum to 8¼ inches square and tape to specialty paper. Add gold tick marks to edges of vellum. Diecut banner from vellum scrap and add title with gold pen.

- Mount stamps on mulberry scraps and adhere with foam tape. String banner with gold thread, hook under brads, and tie with a bow. Adhere finished window to page.

Lieutenant and Mrs. Randolph
Artists: Cary Oliver, Jill Miller
Oval frame: Family Archives
Metallic rub-ons: Craf-T Products
Kraft envelope: Stampington
Specialty paper: K and Company
Corner rounder, circle punch: Marvy

Heritage-Look Frame

Crumpling a pristine embossed frame may call for a bit of courage, but you won't be complaining once you add some metallic rub-ons of sepia-toned ink. This lends an air of antiquity perfect for any heritage layout, as in "Lieutenant and Mrs. Randolph."

❧ From center portion of oval frame, cut a 6-inch rectangle, fold over top of tag and trim as shown. Crumple tag top, envelope, and oval frame, and rub them lightly with metallic rub-ons.

❧ Remove lower button clasp from envelope and adhere it to tag top. Adhere tag top to rectangle cut in previous step. Round off tag corners and mount tag on envelope, restringing button clasps.

❧ Mount framed photo and envelope on specialty paper to complement photo's theme. Circle punch ivory scrap paper and add ephemera if desired. Mount on envelope.

SUBJECT SWITCH
Crumpled frames are perfect accents for other ideas:

· Kids playing in the dirt
· Pictures of Grandma's house (house key or address book in envelope)
· Heritage wedding photos (scrap of bridal lace in envelope)

Distressing Embossed Frames

Crumple frame and rub it lightly with sepia ink pad. Mount photo in frame and wrap both with threads and twine, incorporating the charm. Adhere assembly to page with foam tape for added dimension.

Milford Beach

Artist: Sam Cousins

All papers, tag, frame, stickers:
Carolyn Holt/NRN Designs
Threads, twine: Fibers by the Yard
Sepia-tone ink: Cappuccino
Kaleidocolor Tsukineko
Sun charm: American Tag Company

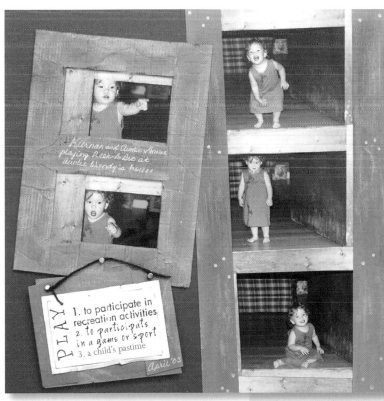

Play with Kiernan

Artists: Shawne Osterman, Jill Miller

Two-window frame: Kreate-A-Frame
Chalk: Craf-T Products
"Play": Defined Stickers by Making Memories
Other: Fine-grade sandpaper, cotton ball, brads, black string

Distressing Cardboard Frames

A touch of sanding and a bit of planned tearing can transform even simple cardboard frames into interesting, informal accents that play off nicely against peek-a-boo photos, shown to great advantage in "Play with Kiernan."

⑥ To simulate rough wood effect, fold and bend frames and peel off small scraps in various directions. Sand frames in one direction with fine-grade sandpaper.

⑥ Using a cotton ball, apply chalk in brown, black, gray, red, and maroon. Repeat crumpling and chalking to create the worn-out effect on the "Play" title box.

TITLE TWIST

- Beach Babe
- Curious Cutie
- Near-Naked Beauty
- Sand in My Skivvies
- Sunset on My Sweetie

Foil Frames

Large black and silver foil panels complement the stark black-and-white tones of the portrait of my niece Shanda in "Shanda Shines." Shanda's blonde highlights pick up on the sunny yellow background paper, the bright lettering, and the little white daisies.

❀ Cut silver foil into two 2½ x 7¼-inch rectangles and black foil into two 7¾ x 1-inch rectangles.

❀ Cut square doily in half, overlap edges so that final photo mat is appropriate to your photo's size, and trim off excess doily.

❀ Arrange foil rectangles beneath doily-framed photo so they act as frames behind it.

❀ Cut out flowers from printed paper and scatter over the composition. Add lettering and adhere all as shown.

Shanda Shines
Artist: Jill Miller
Photographer: Robyn Thornell
Black and silver foil: Amaco
8-inch square doily: Printworks
Specialty paper: Paper Adventures
Lettering diecuts: Sizzix/Ellison

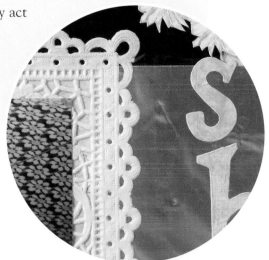

Memories
Artist: Jill Miller
Window cards, 3D diecuts, shaker
frame, stitched paper: Westrim
Seashells, gold wire: MagicScraps
Slide frames: Foofala

Sliding Photo Frame

"Beach Memories" uses small slide mount frames to balance one large sliding photo frame. Take heart—the construction of the eye-catching sliding frame is really quite easy with the use of two window-cut cards, one sandwiched inside the other.

⛵ Place one window card under front face of another window card so that windows are stacked vertically.

⛵ Adhere "Memories" diecut on portion of first sandwiched card that shows through upper window. This will act as a "door stop" when sliding sandwiched card back and forth across page.

⛵ Fill premade shaker frame accent with small seashells and mount in center of lower card window, making sure foam edge of frame aligns against upper card's lower edge.

⛵ With sandwiched card slid all the way to the right, adhere photo within window opening. Slide card to left and mount second photo in upper card's window.

⛵ Add journaling block on left side directly to stitched background paper to act as door stop for lower card. Adhere photos to background paper under upper card as shown.

⛵ Place small photos in slide mounts and adhere to stitched background paper. Secure sliding card ensemble to background only at far right and top edges of upper card so that slider is free to move. Finish with wire accents.

SUBJECT SWITCH

- Around the House
- Friends layout
- Hiking/camping pictures
- Kids in the Classroom
- Travel/vacation photos

CHAPTER 6

Invitation-Style Scrapbooking

Everyone loves to get an invitation to a party. Using invitations, decorative cards, and envelopes invites friends to enjoy the memories you have so lovingly preserved in your scrapbook. These elements also have the added benefit of making your job as family historian a little easier since anything prefabricated aids in the construction process. We'll explore various techniques to customize these premade embellishments so that each and every page can have a homemade touch.

Glassine Envelope

When photos have a distracting background, the composition is often improved by cutting the main element away from the background. This approach works especially well with many floral photographs, as seen in "Friendship Flowers." Extensive journaling cards slipped into glassine envelopes provide a lovely backdrop for silhouette-cut flower photos.

Friendship Flowers
Artist: Jill Miller
Specialty paper: K and Company
Leaves vellum: Autumn Leaves
Glassine envelopes: Stampington
Chalk pencils: Creat-a-color/Savoir Fair
Title laser cut: Deluxe Cuts

Vellum Pockets

"Baby Braiden" capitalizes on two-sided paper for easily coordinated patterned blocking with photo "face" cards that slip into a demure vellum pocket. Experiment with two-sided papers to spice up your scrapbook pages. Here, the strong pastels contrast nicely with the black-and-white photographs, and the bright vellum pocket complements the scheme.

Baby Braiden
Artist: Cary Oliver
Photographer: Shaun Austin
Photography
Two-sided specialty paper, stickers, vellum: Printworks
White paint pen: Sakura

Josh
Artist: Carolyn Holt
Photographer: Diana Payson
Specialty paper, tag, stickers, frame: Carolyn Holt/NRN Designs
Page pebbles, word eyelet: Making Memories
Mini envelope template: Hot Off the Press
Brads: Limited Edition
Other: Gold ribbon

Mini Envelopes

Miniature things have great appeal. In "Josh," Carolyn Holt's use of mini envelopes makes for an adorable scrapbook page of an adorable little boy. The layering effect adds depth to the page, and the watercolor-look specialty paper provides a pleasant echo of the water in the photo.

Overlapping Windows

Not a scrap of background paper can be found anywhere in "Charlotte." Rather, overlapping window cards cover the entire page, making this technique a unique, original idea. Try out different arrangements and combinations of window cards, accented with any number of decorative add-ons—the possibilities are endless.

Charlotte
Artist: Jill Miller
Photographer: Brett South
Window cards, 3D tulip diecuts:
Westrim
Expression sticker: Wordsworth
Lettering diecuts: Sizzix/Ellison
Other: Gold wire, clear vellum,
glue dots, yellow cardstock

Envelope Boxes

Each envelope in "Two Homes" holds postcards of each of my "homelands." The keys in the center add to the symbolism.

☼ Starting with one envelope, fold back top flap onto front of envelope. Repeat with second envelope flap. Position second envelope with front side up under top flap and secure. Repeat with two more envelopes, securing fourth top flap in place on front of envelope. Secure stack to stitched background paper on left side as shown.

☼ Repeat previous steps to build right side stack of envelopes and secure to background.

☼ Remove back of one window card and lay card on top of both envelope stacks as shown. Cut plastic backing slightly larger than window and close box with foam tape. Adhere 3D diecuts and letters diecut from back of window card scrap and heavy textured paper, and layer on background paper with mini glue dots as shown.

Two Homes
Artist: Jill Miller
Paper Bliss envelope-and-card pack, heavy textured paper, 3D diecuts (with plastic backing), stitched paper: Westrim
Lettering diecuts: Sizzix/Ellison
Two gold keys: Home Depot
Mini glue dots: Hermafix

Bubbles

Artist: Jill Miller

Photographer: Shawne Osterman

Gate card: Westrim

Preprinted bubble vellum, glossy cardstock: NRN Designs

Lettering stickers: Provo Craft

Page pebbles, spiral clips, circle tags: Making Memories

Expression diecut: Hot Off the Press

Circle punch: Marvy

Gate Cards

Circle tags make perfect accents for certain themes, as seen in "Bubbles."

❀ Cut a 5-inch circle and a 4½-inch square from vellum. Cut square in half, cut photo in half also, and mount both pieces on gate card. Add journaling and circle tags inside gate card and ornament card with spiral clips. Cut photos into 4½-inch circles and mat photos with larger circles.

❀ Punch smaller circles and adhere them to circle tags. Add lettering stickers and place page pebbles over title letters. Mount all elements as shown.

SUBJECT SWITCH

- Ball playpen photos
- Bathtime photos
- Bubbly personality photos
- Lighter-than-air bouncy toddler photos

Mini Accordion Books

On the surface "Mama's Boys" looks like a lot of work for one small photo, but a foray into the envelope reveals pull-out mini accordion books, made from window cards and filled with photos.

☆ Nest window cards together to create a mini photo album. Invert every other card to alternate the openings, thus allowing pictures to peek through as each page is tuned.

☆ Punch two small holes in middle of album's spine and tie with embroidery floss to create binding.

☆ Tuck flap inside envelope. With craft knife, cut small opening in each envelope to showcase cover photo of each album. Mark position of envelopes on pages and silhouette cut portions of embossed designs that overlap envelope location. Secure envelopes, tucking under cut portions of designs to background paper.

☆ Lightly press ink pad on tags for faux linen finish.

Mama's Boys
Artists: Cary Oliver, Jill Miller
Paper Bliss card-and-envelope pack: Westrim
Embossed paper, teddy bear, lettering stickers: K and Company
Tags: DMD Industries
Linen ink pad: StampaRosa
Other: Yellow embroidery floss, craft knife

Cary Heritage
Artists: Cary Oliver,
Jill Miller
Embossed specialty paper:
K and Company
Gold and copper Brilliance
ink pads: Tsukineko
Text-weight copper paper:
NRN Designs
Decorative photo corner
punch: Marvy
Gold handmade paper:
Savoir-Faire
Leaf spray motif: Jewelcraft
Rose and leaf nailheads:
American Tag Company
Other: Craft knife, bone
folder, gold ribbon

Pillow Pouches

The very elegant background paper of "Cary Heritage" beautifully complements the sepia-tone photograph. The folded pouch takes advantage of the therapeutic nature of folding paper as we watch a new shape emerge with every fold.

- Brush embossed paper with gold and copper inks. Cut out a bouquet motif from upper section of paper (hole will be hidden under photo). Also cut away lower half of central motif at top of paper and mount photo below this cutout.

- Trim copper paper into an 8½-inch square and fold paper diagonally each way. Burnish folds with bone folder. Turn square on point and fold each point into center. (Square will now measure about 6 inches.) Corner punch each point and fold points back into center, again burnishing folds. (Square will now measure about 4¼ inches.)

- Wrap gold ribbon over each punched point, securing ribbon with tape on back and at dead center of square (tape will be covered by journaling square). Adhere leaf charm and bouquet cutout to gold paper, and secure gold paper to top flap of pouch.

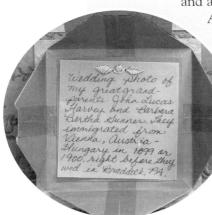

SUBJECT SWITCH
- Antiqued papers are also wonderful for photos of proms, little girls' dress-ups, living legacy tributes, formal functions, and museum settings.

CHAPTER 7

Nine years ago when I began scrapbooking, the only papers I could find to scrap with were white and light-colored solids. Now stores offer row upon row of every kind of solid, metallic, embossed, and preprinted paper imaginable. Paper-backed fabrics are just the latest offering in this very competitive market. The next two chapters barely scratch the surface of the papers available. This chapter explores all sorts of approaches to preprinted paper, with special focus on a popular technique called colorblocking.

Quadrant Layout

Using a preprinted birthday-themed background paper, "Birthday Wishes" illustrates a classic quadrant-style layout. Dividing the page into quarters with ribbons simplifies the layout process.

Birthday Wishes
Artist and photographer: Shawne Osterman
Specialty paper: Wubie Prints
Birthday eyelet letters: Making Memories
Wishes letters: Deluxe Cuts
Square tags: Creative Imaginations
Silver paint pen: Marvy
Other: Ribbon

Preprinted Papers and Colorblocking

Colorblocking

Colorblocking is the art of combining various sizes and styles of paper into blocks of color, pattern, or texture united in a geometric arrangement. If this seems confusing, just check out "Live, Laugh, Love" for a visual definition. The metal words further define the visual division of the page and their curling script echoes the swirls of the decorative papers.

Live, Laugh, Love
Artist: Jill Miller
Photographer: Anita Shell
Photography
3 x 5-inch handmade papers: Savior Faire
Metal words: Creative Imaginations
Expressions sticker: Wordsworth

Preprinted Colorwashed Paper

Vibrant colorwashed paper provides an exciting background for the computer-printed black text of "A Dog's Bill of Rights," a touching reminder of our responsibilities to our pets. The multihued tag ties add a further note of whimsy.

A Dog's Bill of Rights
Artist: Carolyn Holt
Photographer: Todd Ludeman
All papers, stickers, tag: Carolyn Holt/NRN Designs
Threads: Fibers by the Yard
Buckle: American Tag Company

Triangle Pockets

Overlapping a series of graduated triangle folds, all made from a single sheet of vellum, is a clever way to add multiple pockets hidden within a unique mini book, as shown in "Eula Mae."

❀ To make fold-over pockets, fold a 12 x 12-inch piece of vellum in half and then in half again. Turn this 6 x 6 square on point, with folded edges on bottom. Fold top point down to match bottom point. Fold next point down to lie ⅜ inch above bottom point.

❀ Continue folding down points, offsetting each layer by ⅜ inch. Secure all open edges of vellum to create three interior pockets. Fasten surface of bottom pocket to page.

Monochromatic Papers

Black-and-white photos look properly staged when placed against a mottled monochromatic background, as "Snowflake" demonstrates.

☆ Print Snowflakes poem and phrase on transparency and trim as shown. Spray with clear acrylic to prevent ink from smearing. Alternatively, print out words on paper and have a copy center make an overhead transparency from the printout (color overhead transparencies are also available and affordable). If desired, journal in your own handwriting on acetate with permanent ink pen.

☆ Secure threads to torn-edge photo with glue dots as shown. Be sure to tear photo edges toward you to create white edges.

Fun in the Sun
Artist: Cary Oliver
Preprinted color-blocked cardstock, lettering stickers: SEI
Metal-rimmed tags, mini brads: Making Memories
Other: Adhesive tape, double-stick tape

Paper Weaving

Weaving is a very ancient art form practiced with a wide variety of materials. Cary Oliver's "Fun in the Sun" adds a twist to this technique by weaving together striped papers instead of solid ones. The result is an intricate montage of many different-sized blocks of color. Despite the complex look, the technique is not very complicated.

⚓ Cut random widths of 12-inch colorblocked paper. Place half the strips onto white cardstock in a horizontal row. Using adhesive tape, attach only top ⅓ inch of strips to cardstock.

⚓ Tightly weave remaining strips of patterned paper vertically in alternating over-and-under fashion, periodically securing woven strips with double-stick tape. When weaving is complete, adhere perimeter of page to cardstock backing.

⚓ Adorn woven background with photos, photo-accented tags, lettering, and mini brads as shown.

TITLE TWIST
- Cool in the Pool
- Littlest Fishy
- Safe in Our Arms
- Welcome to the Water

Saturday Silliness

Artist: Jill Miller

All papers, snaps, diecuts: Cloud 9 Designs
Mini garden gloves, mini tools: Michaels
Expression sticker: Wordsworth
Gardening sticker: Frances Meyer
Other: Double-stick tape, foam tape, foam core, craft knife, glue dots

Coordinated Sets

Nowadays all the matching components of a scrapbook page can be purchased in a coordinated kit that takes the hassle out of mixing and matching pieces from all over the shelves. "Saturday Silliness" uses every element of a coordinated set to showcase a total of nine photos along with quite a bit of journaling, sentiments, and a no-frills title to boot.

⚙ Stack rock diecuts inside photo frame diecuts and adhere top and bottom rock diecuts to 3¼-inch photos. Crease diecuts to create a photo hinge. Add interior photos as shown.

⚙ Create journaling and title on computer and print them out on text paper. Adhere journaling diecuts over printout with double-stick tape and run paper through printer again. Adhere to background paper with foam tape. Cut out interior of frame diecut for lower mini book.

⚙ Fold paper cut out from photo frame diecut in half for lower mini book and attach miniature shovel with glue dots. Adhere other shovels and attach journaling block to thumb of glove with a snap.

⚙ Cut two rectangles of foam core, one measuring 4½ x 6 inches and the other 3½ x 4½ inches. Remove interiors with craft knife to make ½-inch-wide frame. Adhere ½-inch paper strips cut from background paper over foam core frame.

SUBJECT SWITCH

• Try making hiking, fishing, camping, or personality pages with the poemstones.

advanced

Powdered Metallic Colorblocking

"Lake Arrowhead" is yet another example of colorblocking, but this too is a technique with a twist. A single sheet of cardstock has been divided into various blocks, and each block has been colored, not with papers but with pearlized powders. This is custom colorblocking at its best.

🍂 Arrange photos and expression stickers on cardstock and mark fold lines where elements meet one another. Remove photos and stickers and fold accordingly.

🍂 Sponge one area with VersaMark ink (directly from the pad) and apply one color of Pearl Ex pigments. (Be sure to mask off surrounding areas with paper so sponged color stays only in its designated area.) Repeat VersaMark and Pearl Ex applications until entire surface is colorized as shown.

🍂 Fold each crease back from fold line and brush crease with black pigment ink pad. Brush all outside edges as well. Pick up ink with crumpled tissue and randomly "rag on" black ink all over page. This tones down the powders' intensity and gives an antiqued look.

🍂 Using a VersaMark pen, paint Pearl Ex colors into cells of leaf stickers, cleaning tip after each change of color. Affix photos and stickers as shown.

Lake Arrowhead
Artist: Jill Miller
Photographer: Melody Jones
expression stickers: Serendipity Stamps
Spring green, red russet, and Aztec
gold Pearl Ex metallic
pigments: Jacquard Products
Black pigment ink, VersaMark ink
pad, pen: Tsukineko
Class "A" Peals gold and copper leaf
stickers: Stampendous
Other: Tissues, medium paintbrush,
spray fixative

Entire books have been written on the unique qualities of papers around the world. Handmade and embossed papers are some of the most sought after and elegant papers available, with beautiful designs and interesting textures, and because they are handmade, no two papers are exactly the same. Embossed papers raise their designs to new heights, literally. Mulberry, vellum, fabrics, cardstock, and metals are only some of the materials that have raised designs. It's hard to go wrong when creating pages with such marvelous foundations.

Window Silhouette

Wonderful white embossed paper has a clean, classic appeal. Look for embossed papers with bold motifs that lend themselves to selective cutting. "Cedar Breaks" takes advantage of a snowflake paper to cleverly frame elements on the page.

Cedar Breaks
Artist: Jill Miller
Printed and embossed card-stock: NRN Designs
Other: circle template, craft knife, cutting mat

Embossed Motifs

"Oliver's Fishing Cabin" effectively combines colored, embossed vellum fishes with plaid background paper for a masculine look.

Oliver's Fishing Cabin
Artists: Cary Oliver, Jill Miller
Embossed vellums, printed paper: K and Company
Other: Buttons, black photo corners

Embossed Leather

"Cowboy Spirit" introduces a newly launched embossed material: leather. Tooled leather is striking but very labor intensive. Happily, pre-embossed leather mimics tooled leather without the sweat or the cost.

☆ To frame photo, wrap strips of smooth brown leather around strips of foam tape and secure ends under foam tape with wonder tape. Cover corners with triangles of embossed navy leathers and secure these also with wonder tape.

☆ Mount framed photo and journaling on embossed brown leather. Cut title lettering from tan embossed leather. Add embellishments as shown.

Cowboy Spirit
Artist: Cary Oliver
Photographer: Shaun Austin Photography
Embossed tan, brown, and navy leather, smooth brown and navy leather: K and Company
Lettering template: Cut-It-Up
Other: 1/2-inch foam tape, 1/4-inch wonder tape, ecru vellum

Love and Liberty
Artist: Jill Miller
Embossed paper: Paper Adventures
Heavyweight maroon handmade paper, vellum: Savoir Faire
Other: Embossing stylus, mouse pad, baby's breath, acrylic spray

Layered Vellum

"Love and Liberty" showcases antiqued embossed paper that came straight off the store shelf. With dry embossing vellum you can create your own embossed paper.

♡ Working in the area of embossed paper that will be hidden under photo, cut out two large emblems and one circle with a small emblem inside.

♡ Print journaling on vellum and tear panel with plenty of space above the print to add embossed detail. Place journaled vellum over large emblem and draw over lines with a stylus (place a mouse pad underneath for padding). Fill in entire emblem and adhere small emblem over it (cut from the circle). Adhere circle, framing smaller photo, on lower portion of page and add baby's breath.

McKenna and Johnny
Artist: Jill Miller
Photographer: Beth Olsen
Gold and copper Brilliance ink pads: Tsukineko
Heritage embossed paper: K and Company
Burgundy handmade paper: Savior Faire
Gold bow: Anna Griffin Company
Locket, wire, charms, rose nailheads: Jewelcraft
Banner stencil: C-Thru Ruler
Decoupage medium (optional): US Art Quest
Other: Cardstock to match photo background color, tracing paper

Brushing Ink on Embossed Paper

The elegant background paper of "McKennna and Johnny" is simply embossed paper brushed with copper and gold pigment inks and covered with a glossy decoupage medium.

☾ Mount photo firmly to 5¼-inch square of cardstock. Mask off figure(s) in photo with tracing paper, then sponge gold and copper Brilliance ink over entire surface. Remove mask and let ink dry.

☾ Lightly brush embossed paper with gold and copper Brilliance ink. Brush decoupage medium over all surfaces to seal seams between photo and paper.

☾ Cut 8-inch square from center of 12 x 12-inch piece of paper. Trim off ⅛ inch from all sides of 8-inch square. Cut out 5¾-inch square from center of smaller square (now 7¾-inch square) and rotate 45 degrees.

☾ Mount smaller square onto larger square (now a frame) and mount these over center hole of 12 x 12-inch paper. Mount photo in center of frame. Add decorative elements as shown.

SUBJECT SWITCH

- Heritage photos
- Prom pictures
- Religious occasions
- Weddings/anniversaries

Intermediate

52

Rubbing Ink on Embossed Paper

"Remember When" also uses ink to accent embossed designs but this is a vegetable-oil-based ink that has been rubbed into the papers and stickers.

- ❀ Generously rub red ink into 5½ x 8½-inch sheet of gold paper and border stickers. Rub lightly over red with black ink. Sprinkle black copper and clear embossing powders on gold paper and heat set. Rub inks into background papers as desired.

- ❀ Cut 8 x 10-inch rectangle from center of larger piece of embossed paper. Cut rectangle in half lengthwise and remove embossed design from each piece. Cut only the embossed designs in half again.

- ❀ Adhere all four designs (two to background paper and two to hidden journaling block); trim off excess. Add border stickers as shown.

- ❀ Mount photo centered on 5½ x 8½-inch sheet of inked gold paper. Adhere 8½ x 11-inch cardstock over center hole with foam tape. Adhere only corners of photos, centered on cardstock. Mount all on black cardstock.

Remember When
Artist: Jill Miller
Royal Red and Jet Black VersaFine ink pads, 2 sponge daubers: Tsukineko
Tuscany embossed papers, black cardstock: Club Scrap
Embossed floral borders, clear vellum: K and Company
Glossy gold paper: Card Connection/Michaels
Expression sticker: Serendipity Stamps
Black, copper, and clear embossing powder: Stampendous
Heat gun: Marvy
Other: Scrap cardstock, foam tape

Painting Embossed Paper

"Two Souls" uses pigment ink to enhance embossed vellum. The ink is specially formulated to dry on vellum and is painted on with a foam-tip stylus.

- ♡ Trim vellum to 9-inch square and 3 x 4¼-inch rectangle.

- ♡ Using Fantastix coloring tools (one per color) and Brilliance inks, paint embossed vellum pieces, and paint through lettering stencil onto pink cardstock as shown. Add subtle shading by applying second stroke of ink on flower petals. Apply fabric paint on various dots and allow 30 minutes to dry.

- ♡ Adhere vellum square onto 8½-inch lilac square and 8¾-inch white square. Adhere vellum rectangle onto 2¾ x 4-inch lilac rectangle and 3¼ x 4½-inch white rectangle.

- ♡ Center sentiments sticker on vellum rectangle and set to side of vellum square. Mount all on pink cardstock and decorate with ribbon as shown. Mount photo centered on vellum square.

Two Souls
Artist: Jill Miller
Floral swirl embossed vellum: K and Company
Peacock and Twilight Brilliance ink pads, Fantastix coloring tool: Tsukineko
Calligraphy lettering stencil and pearl fabric paint:
Delta Sentiments sticker: Wordsworth
Other: Pink, white, and lilac cardstock, pink organza ribbon

Painting with Powders

Solid embossed paper offers subtle sophistication, but if you want vibrant colors to pop from the floral design, you can easily paint a single flowering vine with brilliant powders with a pointed, adhesive foam-tip pen. "Magical Moments" shows just how stunning this extra step can be.

☆ Pick up spring green powdered pigment with tip of VersaMark pen and paint all stems and leaves. Wipe off pen tip and pick up duo green-yellow to add highlights on leaves as shown. Clean tip and repeat with duo red-blue and misty lavender on flower petals as shown. Add sparkle gold to dots and diecut letters.

☆ Paint small bird and square frame with duo green-yellow and misty lavender pigments as shown. Spray black groove cardstock with adhesive and sponge all colors in random fashion as shown.

Magical Moments
Artist: Jill Miller
Photographer: Shauna Thalman
VersaMark pen, gold gel pen: Tsukineko
Duo green-yellow, spring green, duo red-blue, sparkle gold, and misty lavender Pearl Ex pigments: Jacquard Products
Floral swirl embossed cardstock and frame stickers: K and Company
Heavyweight vellum, black groove cardstock: NRN Designs
Diecut letters: Deluxe Cuts
Gold mini brads: American Tag Company
Other: Gold wire, craft knife, spray adhesive, sponges

Painting with Metallic Acrylics

"Sealed with a Kiss" is a monochromatic melody of painted brilliant gold and bold brass vellum swirls set against a milk chocolate brown background. The subtle shading of two hues of gold is quite dramatic, yet does not overpower the prized pictures.

⑥ Tear vellum along embossed swirl as shown. Set aside larger piece and tear upper right corner of smaller piece for accent over upper left corner of photo.

⑥ Cut 3¼-inch square from smaller piece and tear remaining section to fit inside book as shown. Paint highlights on swirls with sunset gold Lumiere paint as shown. Paint over all swirls with brass Lumiere paint (the translucent quality of the brass will tone down the intensity of the sunset gold). Dry-brush brass on open spaces of vellum and photo corners.

⑥ For mini book, cut tan paper into two rectangles each measuring 6½ x 3¼ inches and fold them in half. Adhere vellum square to front of book and affix photo corners as shown.

⑥ Layer one 4-inch strip of ribbon down center of vellum and tape on back. Tape second tan rectangle to back of paper to hide ribbon ends. Adhere right side of remaining torn vellum piece to inside right of book and fold book closed to mark inside fold. Adhere remaining 19 inches of ribbon center to center at back of book and secure assembly to page over ribbon crossroads.

Sealed with a Kiss
Artist: Jill Miller

Brass and sunset gold Lumiere metallic acrylic paints:
Jacquard Products
Embossed vellum, specialty papers, lettering stickers, photo corners: K and Company
Gold gel pen, white paint pen: Marvy Uchida
Other: Gold organza ribbon, detail paintbrush

CHAPTER 9

Metallic Touches

Mothers of little men, rejoice. Metal, with all its masculine edginess, offers a way to scrap those manly memories without the quaint and cutesy qualities. And since metal accents take many forms—thick bent-wire words, metal dog tags, metallic creams, foils of all colors, metal meshes and screens— the possibilities are vast. All of these and more are utilized in this chapter, with attention given to concerns about adhesives, reducing bulky profiles, and colorizing metals to soften or enhance its appearance.

Antiquing Cream

Antiquing creams have traditionally been used on carved frames and sculptures because they lend an aged patina to any raised surface. When working with heritage photos, as in "Harvey," the illusion of old weathered and worn surfaces will complete the overall impression of a timeless treasure. To apply, simply use your fingertip to lightly rub any raised surface with a bit of the cream for an instant illusion.

Harvey
Artists: Cary Oliver, Jill Miller
Metallic antiquing creams: Rub-ons Craf-T Products
Fine-tip copper paint pen: Marvy
Pre-embossed frames: C-Thru Ruler
Lettering stencil: Delta
Specialty vellum: Family Archives
Black mat board diecut:
www.thecardladies.com
Other: black organza ribbon, ecru vellum, foam tape

Metal Tag Decorations

I don't know of any parent who hasn't taken these kinds of pictures. Bubblebaths are a favorite activity of children and even some adults too. Since bathtubs and bubbles are usually white, I chose white paper and a preprinted grid vellum to match the background in the photos. Silver metal tags keep everything clean on the scrapbook page—almost as clean as Ian in the pictures!

Bubblebath
Artist: Jill Miller

Metal dog tags: Stampington
Metal rim tags, mini brads: Making Memories
Page pebbles with words: Creative Imaginations
Silver grid paper: NRN Designs

Grandpa's Swingset
Artist: Gary Oliver

Yellow metal paper clips: Staples
Expression vellums: Memories Complete
Lettering stickers: Provo Craft
Other: Foam tape

Paperclip Accents

Use foam tape all along the underside of the large photo mat to make a three-sided shadowbox that will cushion the profile of the paper clips and help to reduce any "bad impressions" they may make on facing pages.

Crane
Artist: Jill Miller
Photographer: Robert Wagner
Blue and black VersaFine ink pads:
Tsukineko
Sponge daubers, silver gel pen:
Tsukineko
Script and silver paper: Card
Connection
Blue vellum, white cardstock, metal
letters: Making Memories
Thistle silhouette paper: What's New,
Ltd.
Sentiments stickers: Serendipity
Stamps
Silver rose Class "A" Peels stickers:
Stampendous
Elastic silver thread (36 inches):
www.thecardladies.com

Metallic Accents

Metallic threads, metal eyelet letters, and silver vinyl stickers become the jewelry on this formal wedding page. Look to gold and silver to increase the drama when dressing up any scrapbook style.

❀ Apply blue ink over script paper with sponge dauber. Sponge a thin layer of black ink in corners of paper and soften with more blue ink on top of black. Write various words over this with silver gel pen. Add lines across paper with silver thread, stringing on metal letters as shown.

❀ Continue sponging inks on edges of white cardstock for photo mat. Mount photo on sponged blue and silver mats as shown. Sponge blue ink on white thistle background paper. Wash hands if necessary.

❀ For mini book, cut 5¼-inch square of blue vellum. Fold square in half and open. Turn square 90 degrees and fold in half again. Open square, turn vellum over, and fold one point to opposite point and open again. (This last fold should be a valley fold instead of the two previous mountain folds). Stop after these three folds. Bring points together so that they meet *under* square diamond front as shown. Add oval rose sticker on front and single roses inside with journaling as shown.

Intermediate

Foil Windows

This diamond shape is a classic pose for a grouping of four. In the empty spaces next to the photo, I drew a motif from the background paper. A charm would also work here.

☆ Cut 7¾-inch diamond from center of specialty paper. Cut 6¼-inch diamond from this cutout. Cut 5⅛-inch square from smaller diamond. Set both frames aside.

☆ Cut foil into 8-inch square and turn on point. Cut 7 x 7-inch plus sign centered in square: place large square specialty frame on top as shown. Center paper and foil elements on background paper over hole. Fold back each flap over paper frame, inserting 4½-inch length of dowel or rolled paper (with 45-degree angled-cut ends) into the fold so foil doesn't lie flat. Secure flaps to frame and background paper with nailheads as shown. Cut corners off second frame and adhere corners at top, bottom, and sides of foil frame as shown. If added dimension is a concern, omit dowels.

Noel

Artist: Jill Miller

Foiled specialty paper: Autumn Leaves
Gold foil (silver on reverse side): Amaco
Diamond nailheads: American Tag Company
Other: Green, red, and gold gel pens; craft knife,
⅛-inch wood dowels or rolled paper

Forever Friends

Artist: Jill Miller

Tangerine, sunbright yellow, sangria, and burro brown Piñata permanent inks; Claro Extender ink refresher: Jacquard Products
Grey stone cardstock, lettering stickers, "Build A Dream" stamp: Club Scrap
Sizzix rectangle frame diecuts: Ellison
Black pigment ink, embossing powder: Ranger Industries
Brass charms, mini copper brads: American Tag Company
Micron hole punch, copper gel pen, heat gun: Marvy Uchida
Other: Window screen, copper thread (1 yard), sponges, plastic plate

Creating with Window Screen

Ordinary window screen (sprayed with de-acidification spray) is another candidate for creative scrapbooking but its dull color may not be to your liking. Permanent inks provide a good solution as apparent in "Forever Friends."

♡ Cut two 1 x 7-inch strips of window screen. Cut one 5¾-inch square of window screen. Sponge all with tangerine and sangria inks. Wrap strips on opposing corners of cardstock as shown and secure on back. Turn square on point and center on page. Secure with mini brads ½ inch from each corner.

♡ Align stamp with corner of one rectangle frame, stamp in black ink, and emboss. Repeat in opposite corner. Sprinkle black embossing powder on other two corners and heat from underneath. Repeat random sprinkle step with second frame.

♡ Mix burro brown and sangria inks and sponge on stamped frame. Sponge second frame with tangerine, sangria, and sunbright yellow. Overlap frames as shown and secure at four inside corners.

♡ Punch 5 holes each side at top and bottom of frame ⅜ inch from each corner, ⅜ inch apart as shown. Adhere inside corners of frame to page over screen. Rub sangria ink onto charms and brads. Secure both charms ½ inch from opposite corners with mini brads. Run thread through charms, frame holes, and brads as shown.

Mesh with Iridescent Foils

"Fall Fun in North Canyon" is a double spread that uses the same maple leaf punch as in "Autumn" (see page 21) to create leaves of foil and metal mesh. Fine wire mesh is soft enough to be punched easily. Flashy iridescent foils are so thin that they must be affixed to cardstock to be punched.

❧ For left page window, fold paper diagonally both ways and cut 9-inch slit on both folds in center of page. Fold each flap back and then fold over just at points to form little squares as shown. Punch squares, diamond fold point to point, and adhere on flaps as shown. Mount copper foil on cardstock with spray adhesive, punch out leaves, and adhere expression sticker on top with trimmed ecru vellum on bottom.

❧ For right page windows, fold paper into quarters and cut one 4 ½-inch long slit, 1⅛ inch from each side of each fold (for a total of six slits). Cut horizontal slit 4½ inches from top left fold, from first to second slit. Cut another horizontal slit 6 inches down from top center fold and last horizontal slit 7½ inches down from top right fold, for a total of three "H" cuts. Fold flaps up and down and cut a 1½-inch slit in each flap end on fold. Fold over each side of flaps cut to form triangle ends as shown. Punch six squares from rust cardstock and diamond fold each point to point each way and lay over flap ends (tucking half of diamond under flap as shown). Add punched leaves.

Fall Fun in North Canyon
Artist: Jill Miller
Photographer: David Thornell
Two-tone tan/brown paper, rust cardstock: Paper Adventures
Wire mesh: Amaco
Iridescent foils: Magicscraps
Dragonfly, maple leaf punch, 1¾-inch square punch: Marvy
Expression sticker: Wordsworth
Other: Glue dots, spray adhesive, ecru vellum

advanced

60

Mesh Collage

"Newport Beach" combines metal mesh and collage-printed vellum with a deep blue colorwashed background reflecting the shimmering surface of the rich blue Pacific Ocean. The basic operations of the computer journaling special effects seen here are fundamental to most word processing programs. These journaling and title boxes were created with Microsoft Word and printed on vellum. For the left-hand page, the headline "Kayaking on the Bay" was designed to read vertically by choosing the desired text direction.

⚓ Begin a new file. Under the "Insert" menu, choose "Text Box." Click on area on your workspace and drag corner to create ½-inch wide by 4-½-inch high box. Click inside box to activate, then under "Format," choose text direction. Click on desired text direction and click "OK." Begin typing in title in Times font at 26-point size.

⚓ Draw another text box 4 inches wide by 4½ inches high connected to the right side of first box. Click inside box to activate and then under "Format" choose text direction. Change text direction as desired and click "OK." Type remaining journaling as desired.

Newport Beach
Artist: Jill Miller

Metal screen: Scrapyard 329
Copper letter stickers: Stampendous
Metal square brads: Making Memories
Copper accent words, expression cutout:
Hot Off the Press
Specialty paper: Wordsworth
Other: Preprinted vellum: Club Scrap

TITLE TWIST
- At the Water's Edge
- Bold Adventurers
- Family that Plays Together, Stays Together
- New Horizons
- Seasoned Sailors

glitter, glass, and Plastic

All three design elements of glitter, glass, and plastic produce a simulated acrylic finish on whatever they cover and each can be used in different ways. Plastic offers almost infinite possibilities, glass adds a sense of formality to anything it covers, and glitter has long endeared itself to many in the crafts market. In this chapter you will see ideas featuring loose glitters, ultra-thick embossing powders, glitter glue, shimmering acrylics, transparency, plate glass, tumbled sea glass, and even plastic wrap!

Tumbled Glass

"Brothers" is a three-dimensional framed project featuring a variety of glass-enhancing products. Inks that dry on glass are used to stencil the title across the glass front. Tumbled sea glass is adhered to a stenciled glass front with silicon glue in a mosaic approach.

Brothers
Artist: Jill Miller
Royal purple, azure, and forest green StaZon inks: Tsukineko
Black wood frame: Michaels
Calligraphy stencil: Wordsworth
Tumbled glass pieces (1 bag): Plaid
Other: Black pen, silicon glue, double-stick tape, kitchen sponge

Snow Cute
Artist: Jeniece Higgins
Iridescent textured snow: Delta
Lettering stencil: Pagerz
Specialty paper, stickers, tag: Carolyn Holt/NRN Designs
Page pebble, snowflake charms: Plaid
Threads: Fibers by the Yard
Crystal Lacquer: Sakura

Glitter Snow

"Snow Cute" uses an unusual design element to replicate glimmering snow: glitter snow texture medium. Be careful to spread this medium thinly to reduce wrinkles in the paper, and back your papers with stiff mat board to carry the weight of the medium.

Superfine Glitter

Loose glitter is readily available in many thicknesses, but the best texture for scrapbookers is superfine because it is nonabrasive. Both "Thornell Wedding Announcement" and "Together John and I" use superfine glitter to accentuate fine details in their vellum backgrounds.

Thornell Wedding Announcement
Artist: Jill Miller
Photographer: David Thornell
Embossed paper, vellum: K and Company
Superfine loose glitter: Delta
Glue pen: Zig
Other: Tan cardstock, palate knife, green organza ribbon

Superfine Glitter with Accents

Real dragonfly wings shimmer with a pearl finish, so nothing less than superfine glitter will do for a truly shimmering scrapbook page. Even the photography has been toned down to produce subtle color that does not detract from the glimmering accents. Applying accents first may seem a bit of a backward approach, but truly there are no mistakes when it comes to expressing your own personal style of scrapbooking.

Together John and I
Artist: Jill Miller
Photographer: David Thornell
Superfine loose glitter: Delta
Together title: Deluxe Cuts
Expression sticker: Wordsworth
Specialty and purple vellums: Autumn Leaves
Tags: Avery
Skeleton leaves: Judikinns
Gold paint pen, dragonfly punch: Marvy

Cracked Faux Glass

The beautiful and unusual effect of cracked faux glass is actually quite easy to create, as seen in "Ian with Cats." A few gold glass beads add further elegance.

☆ Melt layers of ultra-thick embossing powder (UTEE) on top of each other, allow to cool, then gently bend it to achieve cracked faux glass.

☆ Color copy photographs onto mat photo paper and cover with embossing ink. Cover photos with UTEE and heat-emboss. Quickly cover photo with second layer of UTEE before photo cools and heat again. Sprinkle glass beads into hot UTEE as shown (if UTEE cools, simply reheat and try again). Reheat UTEE again and cover with detail embossing powder.

☆ Adhere sticker to green cardstock and repeat process, making sure to cover with UTEE only once and heat slowly. Set eyelets and attach threads as shown. When third layer of UTEE has cooled on diecut (also mounted on green cardstock), apply gentle pressure and bend until UTEE cracks.

Ian with Cats
Artist: Jill Miller
Ultra-thick embossing powder, detail embossing powder: US Art Quest
Clear embossing ink, heat gun: Marvy
Expression sticker: Wordsworth
Gold glass beads: Judikinns
Threads: Fibers by the Yard
Other: Green cardstock

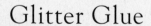

Glitter Glue

The illusion of intricate paper weaving is the primary element of "Jim and Jone" but look more closely to find shimmering highlights, created with clear glitter glues, over the print design.

❀ Cut random widths of 12-inch specialty papers and place half the strips in a horizontal row onto white cardstock. Attach only top ⅓ inch of strips to cardstock with adhesive tape. Tightly weave remaining strips of patterned paper vertically in alternating over-and-under fashion, periodically securing woven strips. When weaving is complete, adhere perimeter of page to cardstock backing.

❀ Add glitter glue to random rows and columns of plaid designs, butterflies, and letters; let dry before adding photos. To create pocket for tag, do not adhere top left of lower panorama picture.

Jim and Jone
Artist: Cary Oliver
Polkadot and plaid specialty paper, stickers, diecuts: K and Company
Iridescent glitter glue: Ranger Industries
Other: Adhesive tape, lilac organza ribbon, clear vellum, lilac eyelet

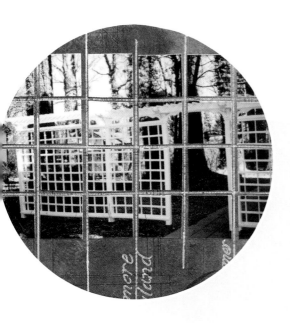

Pearlized Paint

If glitter is too flashy for you, perhaps "Brett's Arbor" is more to your taste. Here, thermography paper has been painted with pearlized paints that feature a subtle shimmer.

SUBJECT SWITCH

- Architecture-themed paper works well for European travel pictures, construction photos, photos of "building a family" or "building our dreams," and children playing with building blocks.

🌀 Stipple thermography paper with various amounts of each paint until all paper is covered. Let dry. Remove paint from embossed designs with tissue. The paint will still come off the embossed areas even though all else has dried, because the paint dries by absorbing into the paper; it does not air-dry like acrylic paints.

🌀 Lightly spray back of one photo with spray adhesive and lay on cutting mat. Using a straightedge, cut apart photo into ¾-inch squares as shown. With white pen draw three horizontal lines ⅞ inch apart, beginning 4½ inches from top of paper. Transfer photo squares onto background paper, adding additional photo splits behind each square.

Brett's Arbor
Artist: Jill Miller
Photographer: Brett South
"Architecture" thermography paper, specialty paper: Club Scrap
Mayan gold, blueberry bliss, and passion flower paint: Radiant Pearls
Stipple brushes: Savoir Faire
White gel pen: Sakura
Other: Tissue, spray adhesive, straightedge, craft knife, cutting mat, photo splits (tape)

Plastic Wrap Water Effects

Look closely at "Waterfall Wishes" and you will see that the river rocks in the background paper really do look like they are underwater. That's not simply the result of a great reality-print paper; it's also an original effect created with plastic wrap and clear liquid glue over a transparency sheet.

☉ Spread out PPA on 12-inch transparency film with a paintbrush and lay plastic wrap over it, crinkling wrap slightly. Allow sheet to dry with plenty of bubbles, then remove plastic wrap.

☉ Overlay transparency on specialty paper and trim excess along rock bed profile. Secure with double-stick tape (it will not show). Journal on transparency rectangles with silver paint pen, overlap ends, and secure under metal plaques with glue dots.

Waterfall Wishes
Artist: Jill Miller
Perfect Paper Adhesive (PPA): US Art Quest
Transparency film: Avery
Specialty paper: Wubie Prints
Corrugated paper: DMD Industries
Metal plaques, letters: Making Memories
Fine-tip silver paint pen: Marvy
Other: Plastic wrap, wide paintbrush, double-stick tape, glue dots

Well-Spent Life
Artist: Jill Miller
Photographer: David Thornell
Embossed vellum: K and Company
Sangria red, tangerine, and sunburst
yellow Piñata inks: Jacquard Products
Transparency film: Avery
Gold metallic vellum: Paper Adventures
Gold handmade paper: Savior Faire
Expression sticker: Wordsworth
Other: 3 kitchen sponges, fine sand-
paper, double-stick tape, mini brads,
permanent ink pen

Inks on Transparency

"Well-Spent Life" also uses a transparency sheet, along with solvent-based inks, to create a stunning backdrop for the photo. These same inks are sponged onto embossed vellum and lightly sanded to accentuate the fall leaves and the finer details of the design.

🌺 Tear vellum along scroll designs. Drop small drops of each ink in an area of vellum and sponge color as desired until all areas of vellum are painted. Repeat process with transparency photo mat and torn square transparency (to be positioned over expression sticker).

🌺 Lightly sand vellum in a circular motion, removing ink from embossed design, and adhere with double-stick tape to background, securing corner with inked mini brads.

🌺 Color copy enlargement of photo onto gold vellum and adhere to page with photo on top and painted transparency underneath. Add journaling with permanent pen. Adhere vellum sticker onto gold handmade paper and adhere torn square of transparency on top.

SUBJECT SWITCH
- Family homestead
- Heritage photos
- Beloved old car or bike
- College-life pictures

Smooshing and squishing things have always appealed to kids and scrapbookers will thrill to revert back to their childhood in this chapter. Not only do we melt puddles into the papers, we puff up some mediums, sand and scrape others, and press and lift all sorts of materials. Filled with fun and frolic, these projects are some of my very favorites.

Hot Glue Stamping

You many smile as much as the children in "Mudpies" when you smoosh a stamp into the hot glue "mud" puddle.

- ⌀ Puddle hot glue onto release paper and press stamp into puddle. Let cool for 30 seconds, remove stamp, and sponge paint with inks.

- ⌀ Stamp half image of emblem on tags and emboss with colored embossing powders. Lay out tags on background paper, mark top and bottom emblem points with pencil, and remove tags. Stamp and emboss emblem on background paper, aligning points with pencil marks. Adhere tags over half of emblems as shown. Stamp and emboss background square with evergreen powder and adhere hot glue emblem and Chinese coins as shown.

Mudpies
Artist: Jill Miller
Photographer: Anita Shell Photography
Gold hot glue: Embossing Arts
Release paper, clear embossing ink, purple and evergreen embossing powder: Ranger
Emblem, "Create" and flourish background stamps: Stampa Rosa
Rainforest green and passion purple Piñata inks: Jacquard Products
Chinese coins: Stampington
Threads: Fibers by the Yard
Tags, photo corners: DMD Industries
Other: 2 kitchen sponges, pencil

TITLE TWIST
- Kids Keep Cool
- Muddy Buddies
- Play the Old-Fashioned Way
- Wish You Were Here

Modeling Paste

To add texture "LaBella Wedding" takes a different tack from Liquid Appliqué. Here, modeling paste mixed with iridescent acrylic paints is used in not one but two ways, one front and center the other a little more faint.

❁ Mix red and blue paints on plastic plate until color is a rich eggplant hue. Add modeling paste but do not mix in thoroughly. Place mesh on right side of white cardstock and spread colored paste over mesh with palate knife. Remove mesh. Adhere painted mesh to silver vellum as shown. Spread paste on watercolor paper to create photo mat and allow to dry. Tear edges when dry.

❁ Cut window opening in painted paper for photo. Cut tag from cutout of photo mat using template. Cut out small square window in mesh for tag. Spread paste over section of mesh and press in metal letters (trim off eyelet loops from top of letters with scissors).

❁ Cut expression sticker in half and adhere top section to torn watercolor paper square. Adhere bottom section to torn vellum (taken from under photo area) and adhere to tag as shown. Mount small photo on small torn square as shown. Add threads and adhere all elements as shown.

LaBella Wedding
Artist: Jill Miller
Magic mesh: Jewelcraft
Ultramarine blue and Pyrrole red Lascaux acrylic paint: Savior Faire
Structura Lascaux modeling paste: Savoir Faire
Silver preprinted vellum: Colorbok
Tag template: Hot Off the Press
Heavyweight watercolor paper: Savior Faire
Expression sticker: Wordsworth
Threads: Fibers by the Yard
Metal letters: Making Memories
Other: Plastic plate, white cardstock, palate knife, craft knife, cutting mat, scissors

Believe
Artist: Jill Miller
Structura Lascaux modeling paste: Savoir Faire
Dark blue Lascaux iridescent acrylic paint: Savoir-Faire
Yellow ochre Jherbin scented ink: Savior Faire
Metal expression, square brads: Creative Imaginations
Expression sticker: Wordsworth
Other: 6-inch length of 2 x 4 wood, ivory cardstock, baby wipes, sandpaper, small mirrors, twine, mesh fabric, palette knife

Faux Weathered Wood

Inspiration can come at anytime. While watching *"The Christopher Lowell Show,"* I saw Christopher demonstrate a faux weathered wood technique, using latex paint applied with a small piece of 2 x 4. I thought, "Why not try that with modeling paste on paper?" I did try it and it is now one of my favorite faux techniques. This scrapbook page, entitled "Believe," is the finished product.

☼ Spread modeling paste and drops of blue paint haphazardly on wood and scrape wood vertically on ivory cardstock. Refresh paste and paint on wood as desired until entire paper is covered (this paper will become photo frame).

☼ Clean off small bits of paste/paint by scraping wood on edges of second piece of ivory cardstock. Add additional paste/paint as necessary to cover all sides as shown. (this will become background paper).

☼ Rub all papers sparingly with a baby wipe that has been dabbed with ink. Add swipes of modeling paste (without paint) as desired.

☼ When first paper is dry, fold over all edges 2 inches and sand folds with sandpaper (this will allow you to tear along each fold with ease). Tear along folds, then fold each side another 2 inches. Sand and tear inside creases to create a square window.

☼ Adhere vellum sticker to torn-out square. Use paste to adhere fabric mesh and mirrors as shown. Punch holes in square and thread twine, knotting each end. Adhere all remaining elements, weaving twine and wrapping ends around brads as shown.

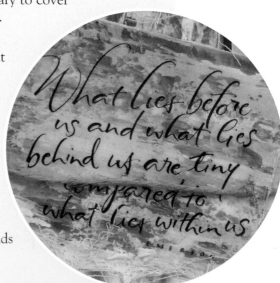

Artist Cement

"Xtreme Soccer" is another spread-and-smoosh technique using artist cement (modeling paste), this time without any color added. The gray tint is the black paper's dye coming through the paste. Experiment with other colors of paper backing to achieve an entirely different look.

- With spatula, apply artist cement to black cardstock (just like frosting a cake). Smooth it all over, allowing some areas to be thick and some to be thin.

- Randomly press stamp into cement and smear sections of impressions to blur image edges. Immediately clean stamp under running water with an old toothbrush.

- Lay metal mesh over cement as desired. Spread cement over mesh to hold it in place. Fold over edges or trim off excess mesh as desired.

- Stamp expression onto small square of black cardstock with white pigment ink and emboss with white powder. Add random swipes of white ink on embossed expression and cut expression apart into line of words (there should be 12 lines total).

- Crop and mount small photos on black mats and mount words around two photos to create borders. Mount remaining single words on scraps from cropped photos and adhere them with foam tape alongside larger photos as shown.

Xtreme Soccer
Artist: Jill Miller
Artist cement: US Art Quest
Large expression stamp: Stampington
White pigment ink, white embossing powder: Colorbox
Metal mesh panel: Scrapyard 329
Metal letters: Making Memories
Other: Spatula, old toothbrush

TITLE TWIST
- Xtreme Aptitude
- Xtreme Concentration
- Xtreme Dedication
- Xtreme Perseverance

Sometimes I get hung up on thinking of the perfect title for a page or finding some creative way to express meaningful memories or hopes and dreams. The following pages are just a few of my solutions to this problem. Titles and journaling are so personal that some of my ideas may mean nothing to you, but many are applicable to a wide variety of themes. Try twisting the techniques to fit your needs.

Creative Lettering

Because I listen to songs while I scrapbook they often seem to get stuck in my head, and I suspect I'm not unusual in this. I love to use song titles and lyrics as titles to my scrapbook pages and this creative crutch has helped me many times, as seen in "Oh Beautiful."

❀ The word "Majesties" is assembled from the "Magical Memories" title. Cut circle off *g* and add small hole punch circle to form letter *j*. Cut out second *s* from perimeter of title traced from first *s*. Use both *e*'s from "Memories" title. Add small crossbar to *l* to make *t* and piece one part of *m* to second *l* traced from first *l* to make *h*.

❀ Adhere all letters and skeleton leaves by running them through a Xyron machine, or use spray adhesive.

Oh Beautiful
Artist: Jill Miller
"Oh Beautiful" and "Magical Memories" titles: Deluxe Cuts
"For purple mountains" lettering stickers, specialty papers: Club Scrap
Moss green velveteen paper: K and Company
Skeleton leaves: JudiKins
Other: Mini copper brads, Xyron machine or spray adhesive

Expressions Art

Expressions Stickers

Another creative crutch is the use of expression stickers to convey treasured sentiments. Touchingly written, these decorative elements add strong graphic appeal wherever you stick them. To me, that's controlled collage, different from random thoughts scattered over the page. The bold design of "Nature's Glory" is achieved by filling in the voids of the photo collage with quite a few expression stickers.

⊙ Trim 1 inch off top and bottom of vellum. Arrange multiple photos of one feature, overlapping edges as necessary on 10 x 12-inch heavyweight vellum. Add computer-journaled column and fill in remaining voids with expression stickers. Adhere three 4 x 6-inch color photos across center horizon of background paper.

⊙ Color copy photos to black-and-white or print digital photos converted to black-and-white with premium black-and-white photo printer (to avoid green cast from color-only printers). Punch squares from various focal points within black-and-white photos for a total of 14 small squares.

⊙ Select any 8-letter words for top and bottom of page (or use the two shown here). Mark center of 1-inch vellum strips and adhere small square centered on mark. Adhere appropriate letter sticker on each side of square, then add more squares, working from center of page outward until both vellum strips are filled. Adhere to page to finish.

Nature's Glory

Artist: Jill Miller

Expression stickers: Creative Imaginations
Metallic lettering stickers: Stampendous
Specialty paper: Wordsworth
Heavyweight vellum: NRN Designs
Stylus Photo 1280 printer: Epson
1 1/2-inch square punch: Marvy

SUBJECT SWITCH

- Children's artwork
- Friendship pages
- Naked toddler pages
- Newborn baby pictures
- Reunion photos

Title Borders

An interesting combination of expression stickers and text editing tricks are apparent in "Proud to Be an American."

♡ Certain versions of Microsoft Word allow you to change text orientation. To design with vertical text (as seen here with "Ian Ford Miller"), create a text box in Word, highlight chosen text, select "text direction" from Format menu, then choose desired direction. The second box containing "I CAN" text is set to normal. In both boxes, opt for no borders and space boxes apart as desired.

♡ Print text on heavyweight vellum. Add expression sticker after printing text. Tear strips of real denim fabric and layer with buttons and small photos as shown.

Proud to Be an American
Artist: Jill Miller
Expression sticker: Creative Imaginations
Denim specialty paper: Carolee's Creations
1 1/2-inch square punch: Marvy Uchida
Heavyweight vellum: NRN Designs
Stylus Photo 1280 printer: Epson
Other: Ripped denim, buttons

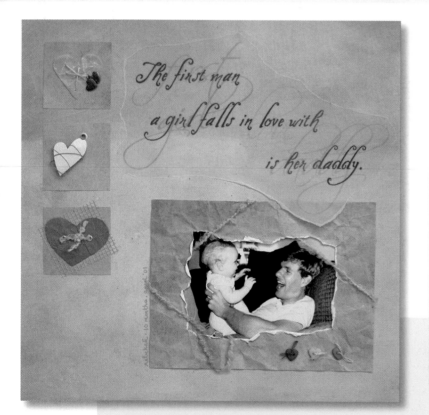

The First Man
Artist: Sheila Doherty
Fonts: CK Elegant, Scriptina
Vellum: Bazzill
Patterned paper: K and Company
Pink paper, fiber, eyelets, wire,
heart tag, floss: Making Memories
Purple mesh: Magic Mesh
Heart charm: Jewelcraft
Other: Spray adhesive, ribbon

Overlapping Text Highlights

Sheila employs some clever text editing features in her word processor to highlight, in a different way, key words in "The First Man." The title for this layout was created using Illustrator, although it can be done in a simple photo-editing program as well.

◖ Type title using CK Elegant in a dark gray font color. Behind those words, type title in again using Scriptina, changing word colors to match paper and making opacity 30 percent.

◖ Print title on vellum and tear edges. Mount with spray adhesive. Add other elements as shown.

My Prayer for Rebekah
Artist: Sheila Doherty
Heavyweight vellum: NRN Designs
Fonts: Gingersnap/Aquiline;
www.2peasinabucket.com
Wooden tag, heart charm:
American Tag Company
Pressed flower: Pressed Petals
Embroidery floss: DMC
Threads: Fibers by the Yard
Other: Burlap, glue dots, cran-
berry red cardstock

Embossing Text

Few people know that you can emboss print with embossing powder right after it comes through the printer! This works especially well with vellum, since the vellum is coated and the ink takes longer to dry. "My Prayer for Rebekah" uses this technique to highlight specific meaningful words in Sheila's wish list for her daughter.

❀ Enlarge digital photo to 8 x 10 inches and add a soft focus through an online photo developer, or scan photo and enlarge and blur edges with photo editing software.

❀ Print journaling on heavyweight vellum. Immediately add embossing powder to highlighted words as they come out of printer and heat set when paper is free. (Be careful not to get powder into printer opening. Wait until text is completely away from opening before covering with powder but do not wait for entire text to print or top of journaling will be too dry to emboss.)

❀ To decorate wooden tag, attach burlap and pressed flower with glue dots. Wrap tag with embroidery floss, threading fibers through tag's hole.

Dreams Remembered
Artist: Jill Miller
Photographer: Epson
Photoshop Elements:
Adobe
Font: Papyrus
12 x 12-inch mat photo
paper: Epson
Heavyweight vellum:
NRN Designs
Rectangle vellum tags:
Making Memories
Other: Buttons, glue dots

Photoshop Effects

Here, advanced editing effects are employed not just with the text on a scrapbook page, but with the photographs as well. "Dreams Remembered" and "Emily Perfect" both use pre-set special effects in Photoshop Elements but are general enough in their execution to be done with other photo-editing software packages. Keep in mind when trying these techniques that there is an endless assortment of pre-set effects and you may just get hooked and want to try them all. You'll begin seeing your photographs in a whole new light.

☆ Enlarge digital photo and position in center of paper. Using polygon lasso, outline one element (in this case the American flag). Choose "Inverse" from Select menu and choose "Conte Crayon" special effect from Effects menu—Image (wait a minute for effect to take place). From Toolbox, choose Type tool and type large word(s) above photo. Then choose "Shadow" special effect from Effects menu—Text (wait another minute). Choose text tool again from Toolbox and type lower script over shadow of larger word(s). Repeat process with lower text under photo.

☆ Print computer text effects and digital photo on mat finish 12 x 12-inch paper with wide-format printer. Print smallest text on vellum. Cut out and mount on vellum tags.